The *Criterion Book*
of *Modern*
American Verse

books by W. H. Auden

*

The *Criterion Book*
of *Modern*
American Verse

Edited with an introduction by

W. H. Auden

CRITERION BOOKS   **NEW YORK**

The land was ours before we were the land's.
She was our land more than a hundred years
Before we were her people. She was ours
In Massachusetts, in Virginia,
But we were England's, still colonials,
Possessing what we still were unpossessed by,
Possessed by what we now no more possessed.
Something we were withholding made us weak
Until we found out that it was ourselves
We were withholding from our land of living,
And forthwith found salvation in surrender.
Such as we were we gave ourselves outright
(The deed of gift was many deeds of war)
To the land vaguely realising westward,
But still unstoried, artless, unenhanced,
Such as she was, such as she would become.

ROBERT FROST: *The Gift Outright*

CONTENTS

I

2

3

INTRODUCTION

One often hears it said that only in this century have the writers of the United States learned to stand on their own feet and be truly American, that, previously, they were slavish imitators of British literature. Applied to the general reading public and academic circles this has a certain amount of truth but, so far as the writers themselves are concerned, it is quite false. From Bryant on there is scarcely one American poet whose work, if unsigned, could be mistaken for that of an Englishman. What English poet, for example, in need of emotive place-names for a serious poem, would have employed, neither local names nor names famous in history or mythology, but names made up by himself as Poe did in *Ulalume*? Would an English poet have received the idea of writing a scientific cosmological prose poem and of prefacing it thus: 'I offer this Book of Truths, not in its character of Truth-teller, but for the Beauty that abounds in its Truth, constituting it true . . . *What I here propound is true*: therefore it cannot die . . . Nevertheless it is as a Poem only that I wish this work to be judged after I am dead.' (Poe, Preface to *Eureka*)?

Maud, *The Song of Hiawatha* and the first edition of *Leaves of Grass* all appeared in the same year, 1855: no two poets could be more unlike each other than Longfellow and Whitman—such diversity is in itself an American phenomenon—yet, when compared with Tennyson, each in his own way shows characteristics of the New World. Tennyson and Longfellow were both highly skilful technicians in conventional forms and both were regarded by their countrymen as the respectable mouthpieces of their age, and yet, how different they are. There is much in Tennyson that Longfellow would never have dared to write, for the peculiar American mixture of Puritan conscience and democratic licence can foster in some cases a genteel horror of the coarse for which no Englishman has felt the need.

On the other hand Longfellow had a curiosity about the whole of European literature compared with which Tennyson, concerned only with the poetry of his own land and the classical authors on whom he was educated, seems provincial. Even if there had been Red Indians roaming the North of Scotland, unsubjugated and unassimilable, one cannot imagine Tennyson sitting down to write a long poem about them and choosing for it a Finnish metre. Leaving aside all questions of style, there is a difference between Tennyson's *Ode on the Death of the Duke of Wellington* and Whitman's elegy for President Lincoln *When lilacs last in the dooryard bloom'd* which is significant. Tennyson, as one would expect from the title of his poem, mourns for a great public official figure, but it would be very hard to guess from the words of Whitman's poem that the man he is talking of was the head of a State; one would naturally think that he was some close personal friend, a private individual.

To take one more example—two poets, contemporaries, both women, both religious, both introverts preoccupied with renunciation—Christina Rossetti and Emily Dickinson; could anyone imagine either of them in the country of the other? When I try to fancy such translations, the only Americans I can possibly imagine as British are minor poets with a turn for light verse like Lowell and Holmes; and the only British poets who could conceivably have been American are eccentrics like Blake and Hopkins.

Normally, in comparing the poetry of two cultures, the obvious and easiest point at which to start is with a comparison of the peculiar characteristics, grammatical, rhetorical, rhythmical, of their respective languages, for even the most formal and elevated styles of poetry are more conditioned by the spoken tongue, the language really used by the men of that country, than by anything else. In the case of British and American poetry, however, this is the most subtle difference of all and the hardest to define. Any Englishman, with a little effort, can learn to pronounce 'the letter *a* in psalm and calm . . . with the sound of *a* in candle', to say *thumb-tacks* instead of *drawing-pins* or twenty-minutes-*of*-one instead of twenty-minutes-*to*-one, and discover that, in the Middle West, *bought* rhymes with *hot*, but he will still be as far from speaking American English, as his Yankee cousin who comes to England will be from speaking the King's. No dramatist in either country who has introduced a character from the other side, has, to my knowledge, been able to make his speech convincing. What the secret of the difference is, I cannot put my finger on; William Carlos Williams, who has thought more than most about this problem, says that 'Pace is one of its most important manifestations' and to this one might add another, Pitch. If undefinable, the difference is, however, immediately recognizable by the ear, even in verse where the formal conventions are the same.

> *He must have had a father and a mother—*
> *In fact I've heard him say so—and a dog,*
> *As a boy should, I venture; and the dog,*
> *Most likely, was the only man who knew him.*
> *A dog, for all I know, is what he needs*
> *As much as anything right here today,*
> *To counsel him about his disillusions,*
> *Old aches, and parturitions of what's coming,—*
> *A dog of orders, an emeritus,*
> *To wag his tail at him when he comes home,*
> *And then to put his paws up on his knees*
> *And say, 'For God's sake, what's it all about?'*

(E. A. ROBINSON, *Ben Jonson Entertains A Man From Stratford*)

Whatever this may owe to Browning, the fingering is quite different and un-British. Again, how American in rhythm as well as in sensibility is this stanza by Robert Frost.

> *But no, I was out for stars:*
> *I would not come in.*
> *I meant not even if asked;*
> *And I hadn't been.*   (*Come in*)

Until quite recently an English writer, like one of any European country, could presuppose two conditions, a nature which was mythologized, humanized, on the whole friendly, and a human society which had become in time, whatever succession of invasions it may have suffered in the past, in race and religion more or less homogeneous and in which most people lived and died in the locality where they were born.

Christianity might have deprived Aphrodite, Apollo, the local genius, of their divinity but as figures for the forces of nature, as a mode of thinking about the creation, they remained valid for poets and their readers alike. Descartes might reduce the non-human universe to a mechanism but the feelings of Europeans about the sun and moon, the cycle of the seasons, the local landscape remained unchanged. Wordsworth might discard the mythological terminology but the kind of relation between nature and man which he described was the same personal one. Even when nineteenth century biology began to trouble men's mind with the thought that the universe might be without moral values, their immediate experience was still of a friendly and lovable nature. Whatever their doubts and convictions about the purpose and significance of the universe as a whole, Tennyson's Lincolnshire or Hardy's Dorset were places where they felt completely at home, landscapes with faces of their own which a human being could recognize and trust.

But in America, neither the size or condition or climate of the continent encourages such intimacy. It is an unforgettable experience for anyone born on the other side of the Atlantic to take a plane journey by night across the United States. Looking down he will see the lights of some town like a last outpost in a darkness stretching for hours ahead, and realize that, even if there is no longer an actual frontier, this is still a continent only partially settled and developed, where human activity seems a tiny thing in comparison to the magnitude of the earth, and the equality of men not some dogma of politics or jurisprudence but a self-evident fact. He will behold a wild nature compared with which the landscapes of Salvator Rosa are as cosy as Arcadia and which cannot possibly be thought of in human or personal terms. If Henry Adams could write:

> 'When Adams was a boy in Boston, the best chemist in the place had probably never heard of Venus except by way of scandal, or of the Virgin except as idolatry. . . . The force of the Virgin was still felt at Lourdes, and seemed to be as potent as X-rays; but in America neither Venus nor Virgin ever had value as force—at most as sentiment. No American had ever been truly afraid of either.'

the reason for this was not simply that the *Mayflower* carried iconophobic dissenters but also that the nature which Americans, even in New England, had every reason to fear could not possibly be imagined as a mother. A white whale whom man can neither understand nor be understood by, whom only a madman like Gabriel can worship, the only relationship with whom is a combat to the death by which a man's courage and skill are tested and judged, or the great buck who answers the poet's prayer for 'someone else additional to him' in *The Most of It* are more apt symbols. Thoreau, who certainly tried his best to become intimate with nature, had to confess

> *I walk in nature still alone*
> *And know no one,*
> *Discern no lineament nor feature*
> *Of any creature.*
> *Though all the firmament*
> *Is o'er me bent,*
> *Yet still I miss the grace*
> *Of an intelligent and kindred face.*
> *I still must seek the friend*
> *Who does with nature blend,*
> *Who is the person in her mask,*
> *He is the man I ask. . . .*

Many poets in the Old World have become disgusted with human civilization but what the earth would be like if the race became extinct they cannot imagine; an American like Robinson Jeffers can quite easily, for he has seen with his own eyes country as yet untouched by history.

In a land which is fully settled, most men must accept their local environment or try to change it by political means; only the exceptionally gifted or adventurous can leave to seek his fortune elsewhere.

In America, on the other hand, to move on and make a fresh start somewhere else is still the normal reaction to dissatisfaction or failure. Such social fluidity has important psychological effects. Since movement involves breaking social and personal ties, the habit creates an attitude towards personal relationships in which impermanence is taken for granted.

One could find no better illustration of the difference between the Old and the New World than the respective conclusions of *Oliver Twist* and *Huckleberry Finn*, the heroes of which are both orphans. When Oliver is at last adopted by Mr. Brownlow, his fondest dream, to have a home, to be surrounded by familiar friendly faces, to receive an education, is realized. Huck is offered adoption too, significantly by a woman not a man, but refuses because he knows she would try to 'civilize' him, and announces his intention to light out by himself for the West; Jim, who has been his 'buddy' in a friendship far closer than any enjoyed by Oliver, is left behind like an old shoe, just as in *Moby Dick* Ishmael becomes a blood-brother of Queequeg and then forgets all about him. Naturally the day-dream of the life-long comrade in adventure often appears in American literature:

> *Camerado, I give you my hand!*
> *I give you my love more precious than money,*
> *I give you myself before preaching or law;*
> *Will you give me yourself? will you come travel with me?*
> *Shall we stick by each other as long as we live?*
>
> (WHITMAN, *Song of the Open Road*)

but no American seriously expects such a dream to come true.

To be able at any time to break with the past, to move and keep on moving lessens the significance not only of the past but also of the future which is reduced to the immediate future, and minimizes the importance of political action. A European may be a conservative who thinks that the right form of society has been discovered already, or a liberal who believes it is in process of being realized, or a revolutionary who thinks that after long dark ages it can now be realized for the first time, but each of them knows that, by reason or force, he must convince the others that he is right; he may be an optimist about the future or a pessimist. None of these terms applies accurately to an American, for his profoundest feeling towards the future is not that it will be better or worse but that it is unpredictable, that all things, good and bad, will change. No failure is irredeemable, no success a final satisfaction. Democracy is the best form of government, not because men will necessarily lead better or happier lives under it, but because it permits constant experiment; a given experiment may fail but the people have a right to make their own mistakes. America has always been a country of amateurs where the professional, that is to say, the man who claims authority as a member of an élite which knows the law in some field or other, is an object of distrust and resentment. (In the field with which we are here concerned, one symptom of this is that curious American phenomenon, the class in 'Creative Writing'.)

> *Amerika, du hast es besser*
> *Als unser Kontinent, der alte,*
> *Hast keine verfallenen Schloesser*
> *Und keine Basalte.*[1]

wrote Goethe, by *Keine Basalte* meaning, I presume, no violent political revolutions. This is a subject about which, in relation to their own histories, the English and the

[1] Things are easier for you, America, than for this old continent of ours; you have no ruins of fortresses, no basalt intrusions.

GOETHE

Americans cherish opposite fictions. Between 1533 and 1688 the English went through a succession of revolutions in which a church was imposed on them by the engines of the State, one king was executed and another deposed, yet they prefer to forget it and pretend that the social structure of England is the product of organic peaceful growth. The Americans on the other hand like to pretend that what was only a successful war of secession was a genuine revolution.[1] There is indeed an American mentality which is new and unique in the world but it is the product less of conscious political action than of nature, of the new and unique environment of the American continent. Even the most revolutionary feature of the Constitution, the separation of Church and State, was a recognition of a condition which had existed since the first settlements were made by various religious denominations whose control of the secular authority could only be local. From the beginning America had been a pluralist state and pluralism is incompatible with an Established Church. The *Basalt* in American history, the Civil War, might indeed be called Counter-Revolution, for it was fought primarily on the issue not of slavery but of unity, that is, not for a freedom but for a limitation on freedom, to ensure that the United States should remain pluralist and not disintegrate into an anarchic heap of fragments. Pluralist and experimental: in place of *verfallene Schloesser* America has ghost towns and the relics of New Jerusalems which failed.

Whatever one may feel about Whitman's poetry, one is bound to admit that he was the first clearly to recognize what the conditions were with which any future American poet would have to come to terms.

'Plenty of songs had been sung—beautiful, matchless songs— adjusted to other lands than these . . . the Old World has had the poems of myths, fictions, feudalism, conquest, caste,

[1] 1829, though bloodless, was a more revolutionary year than 1776.

dynastic wars, and splendid exceptional characters, which have been great; but the New World needs the poems of realities and science and of the democratic average and basic equality. . . . As for native American individuality, the distinctive and ideal type of Western character (as consistent with the operative and even money-making features of United States humanity as chosen knights, gentlemen and warriors were the ideals of the centuries of European feudalism) it has not yet appeared. I have allowed the stress of my poems from beginning to end to bear upon American individuality and assist it—not only because that is a great lesson in Nature, amid all her generalizing laws, but as counterpoise to the levelling tendencies of Democracy.'

The last sentence makes it quite clear that by the 'average' here who was to replace the 'knight' Whitman did not mean the mediocre, but the individual whose 'exceptional character' is not derived from birth, education or occupation, and that he is aware of how difficult it is for such an individual to appear without the encouragement which comes from membership in some *élite*.

What he does not say, and perhaps did not realize, is that, in a democracy, the status of the poet himself is changed. However fantastic, in the light of present-day realities, his notion may be, every European poet, I believe, still instinctively thinks of himself as a 'clerk', a member of a professional brotherhood, with a certain social status irrespective of the number of his readers (in his heart of hearts the audience he desires and expects are those who govern the country), and taking his place in an unbroken historical succession. In the States poets have never had or imagined they had such a status, and it is up to each individual poet to justify his existence by offering a unique product. It would be grossly unjust to assert that there are fewer lovers of poetry in the New World than in the Old—in how many places in the latter could a poet demand and receive a substantial sum for reading his work aloud?—but there is a tendency, perhaps, in the former, for audiences to be drawn rather by a name than a poem, and for a poet, on his side, to demand approval for his work not simply because it is good but because it is *his*. To some degree every American poet feels that the whole responsibility for contemporary poetry has fallen upon his shoulders, that he is a literary aristocracy of one. 'Tradition', wrote Mr. T. S. Eliot in a famous essay, 'cannot be inherited, and if you want it you must obtain it by great labour.' I do not think that any European critic would have said just this. He would not, of course, deny that every poet must work hard but the suggestion in the first half of the sentence that no sense of tradition is acquired except by conscious effort would seem strange to him.

There are advantages and disadvantages in both attitudes. A British poet can take writing more for granted and so write with a lack of strain and over-earnestness. American poetry has many tones, a man talking to himself or one intimate friend, a prophet crying in the wilderness, but the easy-going tone of a man talking to a group of his peers is rare; for a 'serious' poet to write light verse is frowned on in America and if, when he is asked why he writes poetry, he replies, as any European poet would, 'For fun,' his audience will be shocked. (In this Cambridge-on-the-Cam is perhaps a few leagues nearer Gambier, Ohio than is Oxford-on-Thames.) On the other hand a British poet is in much greater danger of becoming lazy, or academic, or irresponsible. (One comes across passages, even in very fine English poets, which make one think: 'Yes, very effective but does he believe what he is saying?': in American poetry such passages are extremely rare.) The first thing that strikes a reader about the best American poets is how utterly unlike each other they are. Where else in the world, for example, could one find seven poets of approximately the same generation so different as Ezra Pound, W. C. Williams, Vachel Lindsay, Marianne Moore, Wallace Stevens, E. E. Cummings and Laura Riding? The danger for the American poet is not of writing like everybody else but of crankiness and a parody of his own manner.[1]

Plato said that when the modes of music change the walls of the city are shaken. It might be truer to say, perhaps, that a change in the modes gives warning of a shaking of the walls in the near future. The social strains which later break out in political action are first experienced by artists as a feeling that the current modes of expression are no longer capable of dealing with their real concerns. Thus, when one thinks of 'modern' painting, music, fiction or poetry, the names which immediately come to mind as its leaders and creators are those of persons who were born roughly between 1870 and 1890 and who began producing their 'new' work before the outbreak of World War I in 1914, and in poetry and fiction, at least, American names are prominent.

When a revolutionary break with the past is necessary it is an advantage not to be too closely identified with any one particular literature or any particular cultural group. Americans like Eliot and Pound, for example, could be as curious about French or Italian poetry as about English and could hear poetry of the past, like the verse of Webster, freshly in a way that for an Englishman, trammelled by traditional notions of Elizabethan blank verse, would have been difficult.

[1] The undeniable appearance in the States during the last fifteen years or so of a certain literary conformity, of a proper and authorized way to write poetry is a new and disquieting symptom, which I cannot pretend to be able to explain fully. The role of the American college as a patron of poets has been discussed a good deal both here and in England. Those who criticize it, often with some reason, fail to suggest a better alternative. It would be nice if the colleges could ask no more from the poets in return for their keep than occasional pieces, a Commencement Day masque or an elegy on a deceased trustee; if that is too much to ask, then the poets themselves should at least demand that they give academic courses in the literature of the dead and refuse to have anything to do with modern literature or courses in writing. There has been a vast output of critical studies in contemporary poetry, some of them first rate, but I do not think that, as a rule, a poet should read or write them.

Further, as Americans, they were already familiar with the dehumanized nature and the social levelling which a technological civilization was about to make universal and with which the European mentality was unprepared to deal. After his visit to America De Tocqueville made a remarkable prophecy about the kind of poetry which a democratic society would produce.

> 'I am persuaded that in the end democracy diverts the imagination from all that is external to man and fixes it on man alone. Democratic nations may amuse themselves for a while with considering the productions of nature, but they are excited in reality only by a survey of themselves . . .
>
> The poets who lived in aristocratic ages have been eminently successful in their delineations of certain incidents in the life of a people or a man; but none of them ever ventured to include within his performances the destinies of mankind, a task which poets writing in democratic ages may attempt . . .
>
> It may be foreseen in like manner that poets living in democratic times will prefer the delineation of passions and ideas to that of persons and achievements. The language, the dress, and the daily actions of men in democracies are repugnant to conceptions of the ideal. . . . This forces the poet constantly to search below the external surface which is palpable to the senses, in order to read the inner soul; and nothing lends itself more to the delineation of the ideal than the scrutiny of the hidden depths in the immaterial nature of man. . . . The destinies of mankind, man himself taken aloof from his country and his age, and standing in the presence of Nature and of God, with his passions, his doubts, his rare prosperities and inconceivable wretchedness, will become the chief, if not the sole, theme of poetry.'

If this be an accurate description of the poetry we call modern, then one might say that America has never known any other kind.

W. H. AUDEN

The *Criterion Book*
of *Modern*
American Verse

Edwin Arlington Robinson

(1869-1935)

MR. FLOOD'S PARTY

Old Eben Flood, climbing alone one night
Over the hill between the town below
And the forsaken upland hermitage
That held as much as he should ever know
On earth again of home, paused warily.
The road was his with not a native near;
And Eben, having leisure, said aloud,
For no man else in Tilbury Town to hear:

'Well, Mr. Flood, we have the harvest moon
Again, and we may not have many more;
The bird is on the wing, the poet says,
And you and I have said it here before.
Drink to the bird.' He raised up to the light
The jug that he had gone so far to fill,
And answered huskily: 'Well, Mr. Flood,
Since you propose it, I believe I will.'

Alone, as if enduring to the end
A valiant armour of scarred hopes outworn,
He stood there in the middle of the road
Like Roland's ghost winding a silent horn.
Below him, in the town among the trees,
Where friends of other days had honoured him,
A phantom salutation of the dead
Rang thinly till old Eben's eyes were dim.

Then, as a mother lays her sleeping child
Down tenderly, fearing it may awake,

EDWIN
ARLING-
TON
ROBIN-
SON

He set the jug down slowly at his feet
With trembling care, knowing that most things break;
And only when assured that on firm earth
It stood, as the uncertain lives of men
Assuredly did not, he paced away,
And with his hand extended paused again:

'Well, Mr. Flood, we have not met like this
In a long time; and many a change has come
To both of us, I fear, since last it was
We had a drop together. Welcome home!'
Convivially returning with himself,
Again he raised the jug up to the light;
And with an acquiescent quaver said:
'Well, Mr. Flood, if you insist, I might.

'Only a very little, Mr. Flood—
For auld lang syne. No more, sir; that will do.'
So, for the time, apparently it did,
And Eben evidently thought so too;
For soon amid the silver loneliness
Of night he lifted up his voice and sang,
Secure, with only two moons listening,
Until the whole harmonious landscape rang—

'For auld lang syne.' The weary throat gave out,
The last word wavered; and the song being done,
He raised again the jug regretfully
And shook his head, and was again alone.
There was not much that was ahead of him,
And there was nothing in the town below—
Where strangers would have shut the many doors
That many friends had opened long ago.

EROS TURANNOS

EDWIN
ARLING-
TON
ROBIN-
SON

She fears him, and will always ask
   What fated her to choose him;
She meets in his engaging mask
   All reasons to refuse him;
But what she meets and what she fears
Are less than are the downward years,
Drawn slowly to the foamless weirs
   Of age, were she to lose him.

Between a blurred sagacity
   That once had power to sound him,
And Love, that will not let him be
   The Judas that she found him,
Her pride assuages her almost,
As if it were alone the cost.—
He sees that he will not be lost,
   And waits and looks around him.

A sense of ocean and old trees
   Envelops and allures him;
Tradition, touching all he sees,
   Beguiles and reassures him;
And all her doubts of what he says
Are dimmed with what she knows of days—
Till even prejudice delays
   And fades, and she secures him.

The falling leaf inaugurates
   The reign of her confusion;
The pounding wave reverberates
   The dirge of her illusion;
And home, where passion lived and died,
Becomes a place where she can hide,
While all the town and harbour side
   Vibrate with her seclusion.

We tell you, tapping on our brows,
  The story as it should be—
As if the story of a house
  Were told, or ever could be;
We'll have no kindly veil between
Her visions and those we have seen—
As if we guessed what hers have been,
  Or what they are or would be.

Meanwhile we do no harm; for they
  That with a god have striven,
Not hearing much of what we say,
  Take what the god has given;
Though like waves breaking it may be,
Or like a changed familiar tree,
Or like a stairway to the sea
  Where down the blind are driven.

CLAVERING

I say no more for Clavering
  Than I should say of him who fails
To bring his wounded vessel home
  When reft of rudder and of sails;

I say no more than I should say
  Of any other one who sees
Too far for guidance of to-day,
  Too near for the eternities.

I think of him as I should think
  Of one who for scant wages played,
And faintly, a flawed instrument
  That fell while it was being made;

I think of him as one who fared,
    Unfaltering and undeceived,
Amid mirages of renown
    And urgings of the unachieved;

I think of him as one who gave
    To Lingard leave to be amused,
And listened with a patient grace
    That we, the wise ones, had refused:

I think of metres that he wrote
    For Cubit, the ophidian guest:
'What Lilith, or Dark Lady' . . . Well.
    Time swallows Cubit with the rest.

I think of last words that he said
    One midnight over Calverly:
'Good-bye—good man.' He was not good;
    So Clavering was wrong, you see.

I wonder what had come to pass
    Could he have borrowed for a spell
The fiery-frantic indolence
    That made a ghost of Leffingwell;

I wonder if he pities us
    Who cautioned him till he was grey
To build his house with ours on earth
    And have an end of yesterday;

I wonder what it was we saw
    To make us think that we were strong;
I wonder if he saw too much,
    Or if he looked one way too long.

But when were thoughts or wonderings
    To ferret out the man within?

27

Why prate of what he seemed to be,
    And all that he might not have been?

He clung to phantoms and to friends,
    And never came to anything.
He left a wreath on Cubit's grave.
    I say no more for Clavering.

THE LONG RACE

Up the old hill to the old house again
Where fifty years ago the friend was young
Who should be waiting somewhere there among
Old things that least remembered most remain,
He toiled on with a pleasure that was pain
To think how soon asunder would be flung
The curtain half a century had hung
Between the two ambitions they had slain.

They dredged an hour for words, and then were done.
'Good-bye! . . . You have the same old weather-vane—
Your little horse that's always on the run.'
And all the way down back to the next train,
Down the old hill to the old road again,
It seemed as if the little horse had won.

LUKE HAVERGAL

Go to the western gate, Luke Havergal,
There where the vines cling crimson on the wall,
And in the twilight wait for what will come.
The leaves will whisper there of her, and some,
Like flying words, will strike you as they fall;
But go, and if you listen, she will call.

Go to the western gate, Luke Havergal—
Luke Havergal.

No, there is not a dawn in eastern skies
To rift the fiery night that's in your eyes;
But there, where western glooms are gathering,
The dark will end the dark, if anything:
God slays himself with every leaf that flies,
And hell is more than half of paradise.
No, there is not a dawn in eastern skies—
In eastern skies.

Out of a grave I come to tell you this,
Out of a grave I come to quench the kiss
That flames upon your forehead with a glow
That binds you to the way that you must go.
Yes, there is yet one way to where she is,
Bitter, but one that faith may never miss.
Out of a grave I come to tell you this—
To tell you this.

There is the western gate, Luke Havergal,
There are the crimson leaves upon the wall.
Go, for the winds are tearing them away,—
Nor think to riddle the dead words they say,
Nor any more to feel them as they fall;
But go, and if you trust her she will call.
There is the western gate, Luke Havergal—
Luke Havergal.

EDWIN
ARLING-
TON
ROBIN-
SON

Edgar Lee Masters

(1869-1950)

JOHN HORACE BURLESON

I won the prize essay at school
Here in the village,
And published a novel before I was twenty-five.
I went to the city for themes and to enrich my art;
There married the banker's daughter,
And later became president of the bank—
Always looking forward to some leisure
To write an epic novel of the war.
Meanwhile friend of the great, and lover of letters,
And host to Matthew Arnold and to Emerson.
An after dinner speaker, writing essays
For local clubs. At last brought here—
My boyhood home, you know—
Not even a little tablet in Chicago
To keep my name alive.
How great it is to write the single line:
'Roll on, thou deep and dark blue Ocean, roll!'

EDITOR WHEDON

To be able to see every side of every question;
To be on every side, to be everything, to be nothing long;
To pervert truth, to ride it for a purpose,
To use great feelings and passions of the human family
For base designs, for cunning ends,
To wear a mask like the Greek actors—
Your eight-page paper—behind which you huddle,

Bawling through the megaphone of big type:
'This is I, the giant.'
Thereby also living the life of a sneak-thief,
Poisoned with the anonymous words
Of your clandestine soul.
To scratch dirt over scandal for money,
And exhume it to the winds for revenge,
Or to sell papers,
Crushing reputations, or bodies, if need be,
To win at any cost, save your own life.
To glory in demoniac power, ditching civilization,
As a paranoiac boy puts a log on the track
And derails the express train.
To be an editor, as I was.
Then to lie here close by the river over the place
Where the sewage flows from the village,
And the empty cans and garbage are dumped,
And abortions are hidden.

PERRY ZOLL

My thanks, friends of the County Scientific Association,
For this modest boulder,
And its little tablet of bronze.
Twice I tried to join your honoured body,
And was rejected,
And when my little brochure
On the intelligence of plants
Began to attract attention
You almost voted me in.
After that I grew beyond the need of you
And your recognition.
Yet I do not reject your memorial stone,
Seeing that I should, in so doing,
Deprive you of honour to yourselves.

J. MILTON MILES

Whenever the Presbyterian bell
Was rung by itself, I knew it as the Presbyterian bell.
But when its sound was mingled
With the sound of the Methodist, the Christian,
The Baptist and the Congregational,
I could no longer distinguish it,
Nor any one from the others, or either of them.
And as many voices called to me in life
Marvel not that I could not tell
The true from the false,
Nor even, at last, the voice that I should have known.

Stephen Crane

(1871-1900)

FOUR POEMS

I

In the desert
I saw a creature, naked, bestial,
Who, squatting upon the ground,
Held his heart in his hands,
And ate of it.
I said, 'Is it good, friend?'
'It is bitter—bitter,' he answered;
'But I like it
Because it is bitter,
And because it is my heart.'

II

Once there came a man
Who said,
'Range me all men of the world in rows.'
And instantly
There was terrific clamour among the people
Against being ranged in rows.
There was a loud quarrel, world-wide.
It endured for ages;
And blood was shed
By those who would not stand in rows,
And by those who pined to stand in rows.
Eventually, the man went to death, weeping.
And those who stayed in bloody scuffle
Knew not the great simplicity.

III

A man said to the universe:
'Sir, I exist!'
'However,' replied the universe,
'The fact has not created in me
A sense of obligation.'

IV

A man adrift on a slim spar
A horizon smaller than the rim of a bottle
Tented waves rearing lashy dark points
The near whine of froth in circles.

God is cold.

The incessant raise and swing of the sea
And growl after growl of crest
The sinkings, green, seething, endless
The upheaval half-completed.

God is cold.

The seas are in the hollow of The Hand;
Oceans may be turned to a spray
Raining down through the stars
Because of a gesture of pity toward a babe.
Oceans may become grey ashes,
Die with a long moan and a roar
Amid the tumult of the fishes
And the cries of the ships,
Because The Hand beckons the mice.
A horizon smaller than a doomed assassin's cap,
Inky, surging tumults
A reeling, drunken sky and no sky
A pale hand sliding from a polished spar.

God is cold.

The puff of a coat imprisoning air:
A face kissing the water-death
A weary slow sway of a lost hand
And the sea, the moving sea, the sea.
                              God is cold.

STEPHEN
CRANE

Trumble Stickney

(1874-1904)

MNEMOSYNE

It's autumn in the country I remember.

How warm a wind blew here about the ways!
And shadows on the hillside lay to slumber
During the long sun-sweetened summer-days.

It's cold abroad the country I remember.

The swallows veering skimmed the golden grain
At midday with a wing aslant and limber;
And yellow cattle browsed upon the plain.

It's empty down the country I remember.

I had a sister lovely in my sight:
Her hair was dark, her eyes were very sombre;
We sang together in the woods at night.

It's lonely in the country I remember.

The babble of our children fills my ears,
And on our hearth I stare the perished ember
To flames that show all starry thro' my tears.

It's dark about the country I remember.

There are the mountains where I lived. The path
Is slushed with cattle-tracks and fallen timber,
The stumps are twisted by the tempests' wrath.

But that I knew these places are my own,
I'd ask how came such wretchedness to cumber
The earth, and I to people it alone.

It rains across the country I remember.

IN AMPEZZO

Only once more and not again—the larches
Shake to the wind their echo, 'Not again,'—
We see, below the sky that over-arches
Heavy and blue, the plain

Between Tofana lying and Cristallo
In meadowy earths above the ringing stream:
Whence interchangeably desire may follow,
Hesitant as in dream,

At sunset, south, by lilac promontories
Under green skies to Italy, or forth
By calms of morning beyond Lavinores
Tyrolward and to north:

As now, this last of latter days, when over
The brownish field by peasants are undone
Some widths of grass, some plots of mountain clover
Under the autumn sun,

With honey-warm perfume that risen lingers
In mazes of low heat, or takes the air,
Passing delicious as a woman's fingers
Passing amid the hair;

When scythes are swishing and the mower's muscle
Spans a repeated crescent to and fro,

Or in dry stalks of corn the sickles rustle,
Tangle, detach and go,

Far thro' the wide blue day and greening meadow
Whose blots of amber beaded are with sheaves,
Whereover pallidly a cloud-shadow
Deadens the earth and leaves:

Whilst high around and near, their heads of iron
Sunken in sky whose azure overlights
Ravine and edges, stand the grey and maron
Desolate Dolomites,—

And older than decay from the small summit
Unfolds a stream of pebbly wreckage down
Under the suns of midday, like some comet
Struck into gravel stone.

Faintly across this gold and amethystine
September, images of summer fade;
And gentle dreams now freshen on the pristine
Viols, awhile unplayed,

Of many a place where lovingly we wander,
More dearly held that quickly we forsake,—
A pine by sullen coasts, an oleander
Reddening on the lake.

And there, each year with more familiar motion,
From many a bird and windy forestries,
Or along shaking fringes of the ocean,
Vapours of music rise.

From many easts the morning gives her splendour;
The shadows fill with colours we forget;
Remembered tints at evening grow tender,
Tarnished with violet.

Let us away! soon sheets of winter metal
On this discoloured mountain-land will close,
While elsewhere Spring-time weaves a crimson petal,
Builds and perfumes a rose.

Away! for here the mountain sinks in gravel.
Let us forget the unhappy site with change,
And go, if only happiness be travel
After the new and strange:—

Unless 't were better to be very single,
To follow some diviner monotone,
And in all beauties, where ourselves commingle,
Love but a love, but one,

Across this shadowy minute of our living,
What time our hearts so magically sing,
To meditate our fever, simply giving
All in a little thing?

Just as here, past yon dumb and melancholy
Sameness of ruin, while the mountains ail,
Summer and sunset-coloured autumn slowly
Dissipate down the vale;

And all these lines along the sky that measure
Sorapis and the rocks of Mezzodì
Crumble by foamy miles into the azure
Mediterranean sea:

Whereas to-day at sunrise, under brambles,
A league above the moss and drying pines
I picked this little—in my hand that trembles—
Parcel of columbines.

LEAVE HIM NOW QUIET

Leave him now quiet by the way
To rest apart.
I know what draws him to the dust alway
And churns him in the builder's lime:
He has the fright of time.
I heard it knocking in his breast
A minute since;
His human eyes did wince,
He stubborned like the massive slaughter beast
And as a thing o'erwhelmed with sound
Stood bolted to the ground.

Leave him, for rest alone can cure—
If cure there be—
This waif upon the sea.
He is of those who slanted the great door
And listened—wretched little lad—
To what they said.

Gertrude Stein

(1874-1946)

Pigeons on the grass alas.

Pigeons on the grass alas.

Short longer grass short longer longer shorter yellow grass

Pigeons large pigeons on the shorter longer yellow grass alas pigeons on the grass.

If they were not pigeons what were they.

If they were not pigeons on the grass alas what were they. He had heard of a third and he asked about it it was a magpie in the sky. If a magpie in the sky on the sky can not cry if the pigeon on the grass alas can alas and to pass the pigeon on the grass alas and the magpie in the sky on the sky and to try and to try alas on the grass alas the pigeon on the grass the pigeon on the grass and alas. They might be very well very well very well they might be they might be very well they might be very well very well they might be.

Let Lucy Lily Lily Lucy Lucy let Lucy Lucy Lily Lily Lily Lily Lily let Lily Lucy Lucy let Lily. Let Lucy Lily.

(from Four Saints in Three Acts)

Susan B.'s voice. We cannot retrace our steps, going forward may be the same as going backwards. We cannot retrace our steps, retrace our steps. All my long life, all my life, we do not retrace our steps, all my long life, but.

(A silence a long silence)

But—we do not retrace our steps, all my long life, and here, here we are here,

in marble and gold, did I say gold, yes I
said gold, in marble and gold and where—
(A silence)
Where is where. In my long life of
effort and strife, dear life, life is strife, in
my long life, it will not come and go, I
tell you so, it will stay it will pay but
(A long silence)
But do I want what we have got, has
it not gone, what made it live, has it not
gone because now it is had, in my long life
in my long life
(Silence)
Life is strife, I was a martyr all my
life not to what I won but to what was
done.
(Silence)
Do you know because I tell you so, or do
you know, do you know.
(Silence)
My long life, my long life.

(from *The Mother of Us All*)

Robert Frost

(1875-1963)

THE OVEN BIRD

There is a singer everyone has heard,
Loud, a mid-summer and a mid-wood bird,
Who makes the solid tree trunks sound again.
He says that leaves are old and that for flowers
Mid-summer is to spring as one to ten.
He says the early petal-fall is past
When pear and cherry bloom went down in showers
On sunny days a moment overcast;
And comes that other fall we name the fall.
He says the highway dust is over all.
The bird would cease and be as other birds
But that he knows in singing not to sing.
The question that he frames in all but words
Is what to make of a diminished thing.

THE PAUPER WITCH OF GRAFTON

Now that they've got it settled whose I be,
I'm going to tell them something they won't like:
They've got it settled wrong and I can prove it.
Flattered I must be to have two towns fighting
To make a present of me to each other.
They don't dispose me, either one of them,
To spare them any trouble. Double trouble's
Always the witch's motto anyway.
I'll double theirs for both of them—you watch me.
They'll find they've got the whole thing to do over,

ROBERT
FROST That is, if facts is what they want to go by.
They set a lot (now don't they?) by a record
Of Arthur Amy's having once been up
For Hog Reeve in March Meeting here in Warren.
I could have told them anytime this twelvemonth
The Arthur Amy I was married to
Couldn't have been the one they say was up
In Warren at March Meeting for the reason
He wa'n't but fifteen at the time they say.
The Arthur Amy I was married to
Voted the only times he ever voted,
Which wasn't many, in the town of Wentworth.
One of the times was when 'twas in the warrant
To see if the town wanted to take over
The tote road to our clearing where we lived.
I'll tell you who'd remember—Heman Lapish.
Their Arthur Amy was the father of mine.
So now they've dragged it through the law courts once
I guess they'd better drag it through again.
Wentworth and Warren's both good towns to live in,
Only I happen to prefer to live
In Wentworth from now on; and when all's said,
Right's right, and the temptation to do right
When I can hurt someone by doing it
Has always been too much for me, it has.
I know of some folks that'd be set up
At having in their town a noted witch:
But most would have to think of the expense
That even I would be. They ought to know
That as a witch I'd often milk a bat
And that'd be enough to last for days.
It's make my position stronger, think,
If I was to consent to give some sign
To make it surer that I was a witch?
It wa'n't no sign, I s'pose, when Mallice Huse
Said that I took him out in his old age
And rode all over everything on him

Until I'd had him worn to skin and bones,
And if I'd left him hitched unblanketed
In front of one Town Hall, I'd left him hitched
In front of every one in Grafton County.
Some cried shame on me not to blanket him,
The poor old man. It would have been all right
If someone hadn't said to gnaw the posts
He stood beside and leave his trade mark on them,
So they could recognize them. Not a post
That they could hear tell of was scarified.
They made him keep on gnawing till he whined.
Then that same smarty someone said to look—
He'd bet Huse was a cribber and had gnawed
The crib he slept in—and as sure's you're born
They found he'd gnawed the four posts of his bed,
All four of them to splinters. What did that prove?
Not that he hadn't gnawed the hitching posts
He said he had besides. Because a horse
Gnaws in the stable ain't no proof to me
He don't gnaw trees and posts and fences too.
But everybody took it for a proof.
I was a strapping girl of twenty then.
The smarty someone who spoiled everything
Was Arthur Amy. You know who he was.
That was the way he started courting me.
He never said much after we were married,
But I mistrusted he was none too proud
Of having interfered in the Huse business.
I guess he found he got more out of me
By having me a witch. Or something happened
To turn him round. He got to saying things
To undo what he'd done and make it right,
Like, 'No, she ain't come back from kiting yet.
Last night was one of her nights out. She's kiting.
She thinks when the wind makes a night of it
She might as well herself.' But he liked best
To let on he was plagued to death with me:

45

ROBERT
FROST If anyone had seen me coming home
Over the ridgepole, 'stride of a broomstick,
As often as he had in the tail of the night,
He guessed they'd know what he had to put up with.
Well, I showed Arthur Amy signs enough
Off from the house as far as we could keep
And from barn smells you can't wash out of ploughed ground
With all the rain and snow of seven years;
And I don't mean just skulls of Rogers' Rangers
On Moosilauke, but woman signs to man,
Only bewitched so I would last him longer.
Up where the trees grow short, the mosses tall,
I made him gather me wet snow berries
On slippery rocks beside a waterfall.
I made him do it for me in the dark.
And he liked everything I made him do.
I hope if he is where he sees me now
He's so far off he can't see what I've come to.
You *can* come down from everything to nothing.
All is, if I'd a-known when I was young
And full of it, that this would be the end,
It doesn't seem as if I'd had the courage
To make so free and kick up in folks' faces.
And I might have, but it doesn't seem as if.

TWO LOOK AT TWO

Love and forgetting might have carried them
A little further up the mountainside
With night so near, but, not much further up.
They must have halted soon in any case
With thoughts of the path back, how rough it was
With rocks and washout, and unsafe in darkness;
When they were halted by a tumbled wall
With barbed-wire binding. They were facing this,

Spending what onward impulse they still had
In one last look the way they must not go,
On up the failing path, where, if a stone
Or earthslide moved at night, it moved itself;
No footstep moved it. 'This is all,' they sighed,
'Good-night to woods.' But not so; there was more.
A doe from round a spruce stood looking at them
Across the wall, as near the wall as they.
She saw them in their field, they her in hers.
The difficulty of seeing what stood still,
Like some up-ended boulder split in two,
Was in her clouded eyes: they saw no fear there.
She seemed to think that two thus they were safe.
Then, as if they were something that, though strange,
She could not trouble her mind with too long,
She sighed and passed unscared along the wall.
'*This*, then, is all. What more is there to ask?'
But no, not yet. A snort to bid them wait.
A buck from round the spruce stood looking at them
Across the wall, as near the wall as they.
This was an antlered buck of lusty nostril,
Not the same doe come back into her place.
He viewed them quizzically with jerks of head,
As if to ask, 'Why don't you make some motion?
Or give some sign of life? Because you can't.
I doubt if you're as living as you look.'
This till he had them almost feeling dared
To stretch a proffering hand—and a spell-breaking.
Then he too passed unscared along the wall.
Two had seen two, whichever side you spoke from.
'This *must* be all.' It was all. Still they stood,
A great wave from it going over them,
As if the earth in one unlooked-for favour
Had made them certain earth returned their love.

NEITHER OUT FAR NOR IN DEEP

The people along the sand
All turn and look one way.
They turn their back on the land.
They look at the sea all day.

As long as it takes to pass
A ship keeps raising its hull;
The wetter ground like glass
Reflects a standing gull.

The land may vary more;
But wherever the truth may be—
The water comes ashore,
And the people look at the sea.

They cannot look out far.
They cannot look in deep.
But when was that ever a bar
To any watch they keep?

DESIGN

I found a dimpled spider, fat and white,
On a white heal-all, holding up a moth
Like a white piece of rigid satin cloth—
Assorted characters of death and blight
Mixed ready to begin the morning right,
Like the ingredients of a witches' broth—
A snow-drop spider, a flower like a froth,
And dead wings carried like a paper kite.

What had that flower to do with being white,
The wayside blue and innocent heal-all?

What brought the kindred spider to that height,
Then steered the white moth thither in the night?
What but design of darkness to appal?—
If design govern in a thing so small.

THE MOST OF IT

He thought he kept the universe alone;
For all the voice in answer he could wake
Was but the mocking echo of his own
From some tree-hidden cliff across the lake.
Some morning from the boulder-broken beach
He would cry out on life, that what it wants
Is not its own love back in copy speech,
But counter-love, original response.
And nothing ever came of what he cried
Unless it was the embodiment that crashed
In the cliff's talus on the other side,
And then in the far distant water splashed,
But after a time allowed for it to swim,
Instead of proving human when it neared
And someone else additional to him,
As a great buck it powerfully appeared,
Pushing the crumpled water up ahead,
And landed pouring like a waterfall,
And stumbled through the rocks with horny tread,
And forced the underbrush—and that was all.

NEVER AGAIN WOULD BIRDS' SONG BE THE SAME

He would declare and could himself believe
That the birds there in all the garden round
From having heard the daylong voice of Eve
Had added to their own an oversound,
Her tone of meaning but without the words.
Admittedly an eloquence so soft
Could only have had an influence on birds
When call or laughter carried it aloft.
Be that as may be, she was in their song.
Moreover her voice upon their voices crossed
Had now persisted in the woods so long
That probably it never would be lost.
Never again would birds' song be the same.
And to do that to birds was why she came.

THE MIDDLENESS OF THE ROAD

The road at the top of the rise
Seems to come to an end
And take off into the skies.
So at the distant bend

It seems to go into a wood,
The place of standing still
As long the trees have stood.
But say what Fancy will,

The mineral drops that explode
To drive my ton of car
Are limited to the road.
They deal with near and far,

But have almost nothing to do
With the absolute flight and rest
The universal blue
And local green suggest.

ROBERT
FROST

DIRECTIVE

Back out of all this now too much for us,
Back in a time made simple by the loss
Of detail, burned, dissolved, and broken off
Like graveyard marble sculpture in the weather,
There is a house that is no more a house
Upon a farm that is no more a farm
And in a town that is no more a town.
The road there, if you'll let a guide direct you
Who only has at heart your getting lost,
May seem as if it should have been a quarry—
Great monolithic knees the former town
Long since gave up pretence of keeping covered.
And there's a story in a book about it:
Besides the wear of iron wagon wheels
The ledges show lines ruled southeast northwest,
The chisel work of an enormous Glacier
That braced his feet against the Arctic Pole.
You must not mind a certain coolness from him
Still said to haunt this side of Panther Mountain.
Nor need you mind the serial ordeal
Of being watched from forty cellar holes
As if by eye pairs out of forty firkins.
As for the woods' excitement over you
That sends light rustle rushes to their leaves,
Charge that to upstart inexperience.
Where were they all not twenty years ago ?
They think too much of having shaded out
A few old pecker-fretted apple trees.

ROBERT
FROST
Make yourself up a cheering song of how
Someone's road home from work this once was,
Who may be just ahead of you on foot
Or creaking with a buggy load of grain.
The height of the adventure is the height
Of country where two village cultures faded
Into each other. Both of them are lost.
And if you're lost enough to find yourself
By now, pull in your ladder road behind you
And put a sign up CLOSED to all but me.
Then make yourself at home. The only field
Now left's no bigger than a harness gall.
First there's the children's house of make believe,
Some shattered dishes underneath a pine,
The playthings in the playhouse of the children.
Weep for what little things could make them glad.
Then for the house that is no more a house,
But only a belilaced cellar hole,
Now slowly closing like a dent in dough.
This was no playhouse but a house in earnest.
Your destination and your destiny's
A brook that was the water of the house,
Cold as a spring as yet so near its source,
Too lofty and original to rage.
(We know the valley streams that when aroused
Will leave their tatters hung on barb and thorn.)
I have kept hidden in the instep arch
Of an old cedar at the waterside
A broken drinking goblet like the Grail
Under a spell so the wrong ones can't find it,
So can't get saved, as Saint Mark says they mustn't.
(I stole the goblet from the children's playhouse.)
Here are your waters and your watering place.
Drink and be whole again beyond confusion.

Don Marquis

(1878-1937)

archys autobiography

if all the verse what i have wrote
were boiled together in a kettle
twould make a meal for every goat
from nome to popocatapetl
mexico

and all the prose what i have penned
if laid together end to end
would reach from russia to south bend
indiana

but all the money what i saved
from all them works at which i slaved
is not enough to get me shaved
every morning

and all the dams which i care
if heaped together in the air
would not reach much of anywhere
they wouldnt

because i dont shave every day
and i write for arts sake anyway
and always hate to take my pay
i loathe it

and all of you who credit that
could sit down on an opera hat
and never crush the darn thing flat
you skeptics

archy

archys last name

boss i just discovered what
my last name is i
pass it on to you i belong to the
family of the blattidæ right o
said mehitabel the cat when i told her
about it they have
got you sized up right you blatt out
everything you hear
i gleaned the information from
a bulletin issued by the
united states department of
agriculture which you left on the
floor by your desk it was entitled
cockroaches and written by
e l marlatt entomologist and acting
chief in the absence of the chief and he
tells a dozen ways of killing roaches boss
what business has the united states
government got
to sick a high salaried
expert onto a poor little roach
please leave me some
more cheerful literature also please
get your typewriter fixed the keys are
working hard again butting them as i
do one at a time with
my head i get awful pains in my
neck writing for you

archy

artists shouldnt have offspring

DON
MARQUIS

*A bulletin from Archy the Cockroach, who started out last July to
hitch-hike from Hollywood to New York with Mehitabel the Cat and
Mehitabel's seven platinum-blonde kittens :*

had a great ride boss
got a ride on the running board of a car
and caught up with mehitabel
in new mexico where she is gadding about
with a coyote friend
i asked her where the kittens were
kittens said mehitabel kittens
with a puzzled look on her face
why goodness gracious i seem to remember
that i did have some kittens
i hope nothing terrible has happened
to the poor little things but if something has
i suppose they are better off
an artist like me shouldnt really
have offspring it handicaps her career
archy i want you to meet my boy friend
cowboy bill the coyote i call him
i am trying to get him to come to new york
with me and do a burlesque turn
isnt he handsome i said tactfully that he looked
very distinguished to me and all bill said
was nerts insect nerts

archy

Carl Sandburg

(1878-   )

PERSONALITY

Musings of a Police Reporter in the Identification Bureau

You have loved forty women, but you have only one thumb.
You have led a hundred secret lives, but you mark only one
thumb.
You go round the world and fight in a thousand wars and
win all the world's honours, but when you come back
home the print of the one thumb your mother gave
you is the same print of thumb you had in the old
home when your mother kissed you and said good-bye.
Out of the whirling womb of time come millions of men and
their feet crowd the earth and they cut one another's
throats for room to stand and among them all are not
two thumbs alike.
Somewhere is a Great God of Thumbs who can tell the
inside story of this.

CLOCKS

Here is a face that says half-past seven the same way whether
a murder or a wedding goes on, whether a funeral or a
picnic crowd passes.
A tall one I know at the end of a hallway broods in shadows
and is watching booze eat out the insides of the man of
the house; it has seen five hopes go in five years: one
woman, one child, and three dreams.

A little one carried in a leather box by an actress rides with CARL SAND-BURG her to hotels and is under her pillow in a sleeping-car between one-night stands.

One hoists a phiz over a railroad station; it points numbers to people a quarter-mile away who believe it when other clocks fail.

And of course . . . there are wrist watches over the pulses of airmen eager to go to France. . . .

BAS-RELIEF

Five geese deploy mysteriously.
Onward proudly with flagstaffs,
Hearses with silver bugles,
Bushels of plum-blossoms dropping
For ten mystic web-feet—
Each his own drum-major,
Each charged with the honour
Of the ancient goose nation,
Each with a nose-length surpassing
The nose-lengths of rival nations.
Sombrely, slowly, unimpeachably,
Five geese deploy mysteriously.

Vachel Lindsay

(1879-1931)

THE FLUTE OF THE LONELY

(To the tune of 'Gaily the Troubadour')

Faintly the ne'er-do-well
Breathed through his flute:
All the tired neighbour-folk,
Hearing, were mute.
In their neat doorways sat,
Labours all done,
Helpless, relaxed, o'er-wrought,
Evening begun.

None of them there beguiled
Work-thoughts away,
Like to this reckless, wild
Loafer by day.
(Weeds in his flowers upgrown!
Fences awry!
Rubbish and bottles heaped!
Yard like a sty!)

There in his lonely door,
Leering and lean,
Staggering, liquor-stained,
Outlawed, obscene—
Played he his moonlight thought,
Mastered his flute.
All the tired neighbour-folk,
Hearing, were mute.
None but he, in that block,

Knew such a tune.
All loved the strain, and all
Looked at the moon!

WHAT THE MOON SAW

Two statesmen met by moonlight.
Their ease was partly feigned.
They glanced about the prairie.
Their faces were constrained.
In various ways aforetime
They had misled the state,
Yet did it so politely
Their henchmen thought them great.
They sat beneath a hedge and spake
No word, but had a smoke.
A satchel passed from hand to hand.
Next day, the deadlock broke.

BRYAN, BRYAN, BRYAN, BRYAN

*The campaign of eighteen ninety-six, as viewed at the time by a
sixteen-year-old, etc.*

I

In a nation of one hundred fine, mob-hearted, lynching,
    relenting, repenting millions,
There are plenty of sweeping, swinging, stinging, gorgeous
    things to shout about,
And knock your old blue devils out.

I brag and chant of Bryan, Bryan, Bryan,
Candidate for president who sketched a silver Zion,
The one American Poet who could sing outdoors,

VACHEL
LINDSAY He brought in tides of wonder, of unprecedented splendour,
Wild roses from the plains, that made hearts tender,
All the funny circus silks
Of politics unfurled,
Bartlett pears of romance that were honey at the cores,
And torchlights down the street, to the end of the world.

There were truths eternal in the gab and tittle-tattle.
There were real heads broken in the fustian and the rattle.
There were real lines drawn:
Not the silver and the gold,
But Nebraska's cry went eastward against the dour and old,
The mean and cold.

It was eighteen ninety-six, and I was just sixteen
And Altgeld ruled in Springfield, Illinois,
When there came from the sunset Nebraska's shout of joy:
In a coat like a deacon, in a black Stetson hat
He scourged the elephant plutocrats
With barbed wire from the Platte.
The scales dropped from their mighty eyes.
They saw that summer's noon
A tribe of wonders coming
To a marching tune.

Oh, the longhorns from Texas,
The jay hawks from Kansas,
The plop-eyed bungaroo and giant giassicus,
The varmint, chipmunk, bugaboo,
The horned-toad, prairie-dog and ballyhoo,
From all the newborn states arow,

Bidding the eagles of the west fly on,
Bidding the eagles of the west fly on.
The fawn, prodactyl and thing-a-ma-jig,
The rakaboor, the hellangone,
The whangdoodle, batfowl and pig,

The coyote, wild-cat and grizzly in a glow,
In a miracle of health and speed, the whole breed abreast,
They leaped the Mississippi, blue border of the West,
From the Gulf to Canada, two thousand miles long:—
Against the towns of Tubal Cain,
Ah,—sharp was their song.
Against the ways of Tubal Cain, too cunning for the young,
The longhorn calf, the buffalo and wampus gave tongue.

These creatures were defending things Mark Hanna never
        dreamed:
The moods of airy childhood that in desert dews gleamed,
The gossamers and whimsies,
The monkeyshines and didoes
Rank and strange
Of the canyons and the range,
The ultimate fantastics

Of the far western slope,
And of prairie schooner children
Born beneath the stars,
Beneath falling snows,
Of the babies born at midnight
In the sod huts of lost hope,
With no physician there,
Except a Kansas prayer,
With the Indian raid a howling through the air.
And all these in their helpless days
By the dour East oppressed,
Mean paternalism
Making their mistakes for them,
Crucifying half the West,
Till the whole Atlantic coast
Seemed a giant spider's nest.

And these children and their sons
At last rode through the cactus,

A cliff of mighty cowboys
On the lope,
With gun and rope.
And all the way to frightened Maine the old East heard them
    call,
And saw our Bryan by a mile lead the wall
Of men and whirling flowers and beasts,
The bard and the prophet of them all.
Prairie avenger, mountain lion,
Bryan, Bryan, Bryan, Bryan,
Gigantic troubadour, speaking like a siege gun,
Smashing Plymouth Rock with his boulders from the West,
And just a hundred miles behind, tornadoes piled across the
    sky,
Blotting out sun and moon,
A sign on high.

Headlong, dazed and blinking in the weird green light,
The scalawags made moan, afraid to fight.

II

When Bryan came to Springfield, and Altgeld gave him
    greeting,
Rochester was deserted, Divernon was deserted,
Mechanicsburg, Riverton, Chickenbristle, Cotton Hill,
Empty: for all Sangamon drove to the meeting—
In silver-decked racing cart,
Buggy, buckboard, carryall,
Carriage, phaeton, whatever would haul,
And silver-decked farm-wagons gritted, banged and rolled,
With the new tale of Bryan by the iron tires told.

The State House loomed afar,
A speck, a hive, a football,
A captive balloon!

And the town was all one spreading wing of bunting, plumes, VACHEL
  and sunshine, LINDSAY
Every rag and flag, and Bryan picture sold,
When the rigs in many a dusty line
Jammed our streets at noon,
And joined the wild parade against the power of gold.

We roamed, we boys from High School,
With mankind,
While Springfield gleamed,
Silk-lined.
Oh, Tom Dines, and Art Fitzgerald,
And the gangs that they could get!
I can hear them yelling yet.
Helping the incantation,
Defying aristocracy,
With every bridle gone,

Ridding the world of the low down mean,
Bidding the eagles of the West fly on,
Bidding the eagles of the West fly on,
We were bully, wild and woolly,
Never yet curried below the knees.
We saw flowers in the air,
Fair as the Pleiades, bright as Orion,
—Hopes of all mankind,
Made rare, resistless, thrice refined.
Oh, we bucks from every Springfield ward!
Colts of democracy—
Yet time-winds out of Chaos from the star-fields of the Lord.

The long parade rolled on. I stood by my best girl.
She was a cool young citizen, with wise and laughing eyes.
With my necktie by my ear, I was stepping on my dear,
But she kept like a pattern, without a shaken curl.

She wore in her hair a brave prairie rose.
Her gold chums cut her, for that was not the pose.

No Gibson Girl would wear it in that fresh way.
But we were fairy Democrats, and this was our day.

The earth rocked like the ocean, the sidewalk was a deck.
The houses for the moment were lost in the wide wreck.
And the bands played strange and stranger music as they
 trailed along.
Against the ways of Tubal Cain,
Ah, sharp was their song!
The demons in the bricks, the demons in the grass,
The demons in the bank-vaults peered out to see us pass,
And the angels in the trees, the angels in the grass,
The angels in the flags, peered out to see us pass.
And the sidewalk was our chariot, and the flowers bloomed
 higher,
And the street turned to silver and the grass turned to fire,
And then it was but grass, and the town was there again,
A place for women and men.

III

Then we stood where we could see
Every band,
And the speaker's stand.
And Bryan took the platform.
And he was introduced.
And he lifted his hand
And cast a new spell.
Progressive silence fell
In Springfield,
In Illinois,
Around the world.
Then we heard these glacial boulders across the prairie
 rolled:
'The people have a right to make their own mistakes . . .
You shall not crucify mankind
Upon a cross of gold.'

And everybody heard him—
In the streets and State House yard.
And everybody heard him
In Springfield, in Illinois,
Around and around and around the world,
That danced upon its axis
And like a darling broncho whirled.

IV

July, August, suspense.
Wall Street lost to sense.
August, September, October,
More suspense,
And the whole East down like a wind-smashed fence.

Then Hanna to the rescue,
Hanna of Ohio,
Rallying the roller-tops,
Rallying the bucket-shops.
Threatening drouth and death
Promising manna,
Rallying the trusts against the bawling flannelmouth;
Invading misers' cellars,

Tin-cans, socks,
Melting down the rocks,
Pouring out the long green to a million workers,
Spondulix by the mountain-load, to stop each new tornado,
And beat the cheapskate, blatherskite,
Populistic, anarchistic,
Deacon—desperado.

V

Election night at midnight:
Boy Bryan's defeat.
Defeat of western silver.

VACHEL LINDSAY Defeat of the wheat.
Victory of letterfiles
And plutocrats in miles
With dollar signs upon their coats,
Diamond watchchains on their vests
And spats on their feet.
Victory of custodians,
Plymouth Rock,
And all that inbred landlord stock.
Victory of the neat.
Defeat of the aspen groves of Colorado valleys,
The blue bells of the Rockies,
And blue bonnets of old Texas,
By the Pittsburg alleys.
Defeat of alfalfa and the Mariposa lily.
Defeat of the Pacific and the long Mississippi.
Defeat of the young by the old and silly.
Defeat of tornadoes by the poison vats supreme.
Defeat of my boyhood, defeat of my dream.

VI

Where is McKinley, that respectable McKinley,
The man without an angle or a tangle,
Who soothed down the city man and soothed down the
farmer,
The German, the Irish, the Southerner, the Northerner,
Who climbed every greasy pole, and slipped through every
crack;
Who soothed down the gambling hall, the bar-room, the
church,
The devil vote, the angel vote, the neutral vote,
The desperately wicked, and their victims on the rack,
The gold vote, the silver vote, the brass vote, the lead vote,
Every vote? . . .
Where is McKinley, Mark Hanna's McKinley,
His slave, his echo, his suit of clothes?

Gone to join the shadows, with the pomps of that time,
And the flame of that summer's prairie rose.

Where is Cleveland whom the Democratic platform
Read from the party in a glorious hour,
Gone to join the shadows with pitchfork Tillman,
And sledge-hammer Altgeld who wrecked his power.

Where is Hanna, bulldog Hanna.
Low-browed Hanna, who said: 'Stand pat'?
Gone to his place with old Pierpont Morgan.
Gone somewhere . . . with lean rat Platt.

Where is Roosevelt, the young dude cowboy,
Who hated Bryan, then aped his way?
Gone to join the shadows with mighty Cromwell
And tall King Saul, till the Judgment day.

Where is Altgeld, brave as the truth,
Whose name the few still say with tears?
Gone to join the ironies with Old John Brown,
Whose fame rings loud for a thousand years.

Where is that boy, that Heaven-born Bryan,
That Homer Bryan, who sang from the West?
Gone to join the shadows with Altgeld the Eagle,
Where the kings and the slaves and the troubadours rest.

FACTORY WINDOWS ARE ALWAYS BROKEN

Factory windows are always broken.
Somebody's always throwing bricks,
Somebody's always heaving cinders,
Playing ugly Yahoo tricks.

67

VACHEL LINDSAY

Factory windows are always broken.
Other windows are let alone.
No one throws through the chapel-window
The bitter, snarling derisive stone.

Factory windows are always broken.
Something or other is going wrong.
Something is rotten—I think, in Denmark.
End of the factory-window song.

Wallace Stevens

(1879-1955)

THE SNOW MAN

One must have a mind of winter
To regard the frost and the boughs
Of the pine-trees crusted with snow;

And have been cold a long time
To behold the junipers shagged with ice,
The spruces rough in the distant glitter

Of the January sun; and not to think
Of any misery in the sound of the wind,
In the sound of a few leaves,

Which is the sound of the land
Full of the same wind
That is blowing in the same bare place

For the listener, who listens in the snow,
And, nothing himself, beholds
Nothing that is not there and the nothing that is.

DISILLUSIONMENT OF TEN O'CLOCK

The houses are haunted
By white night-gowns.
None are green,
Or purple with green rings,
Or green with yellow rings,

Or yellow with blue rings.
None of them are strange,
With socks of lace
And beaded ceintures.
People are not going
To dream of baboons and periwinkles.
Only, here and there, an old sailor,
Drunk and asleep in his boots,
Catches tigers
In red weather.

SUNDAY MORNING

Complacencies of the peignoir, and late
Coffee and oranges in a sunny chair,
And the green freedom of a cockatoo
Upon a rug mingle to dissipate
The holy hush of ancient sacrifice.
She dreams a little, and she feels the dark
Encroachment of that old catastrophe,
As a calm darkens among water-lights.
The pungent oranges and bright, green wings
Seem things in some procession of the dead,
Winding across wide water, without sound.
The day is like wide water, without sound,
Stilled for the passing of her dreaming feet
Over the seas, to silent Palestine,
Dominion of the blood and sepulchre.

II

Why should she give her bounty to the dead?
What is divinity if it can come
Only in silent shadows and in dreams?

Shall she not find in comforts of the sun,
In pungent fruit and bright, green wings, or else
In any balm or beauty of the earth,
Things to be cherished like the thought of heaven?
Divinity must live within herself:
Passions of rain, or moods in falling snow;
Grievings in loneliness, or unsubdued
Elations when the forest blooms; gusty
Emotions on wet roads on autumn nights;
All pleasures and all pains, remembering
The bough of summer and the winter branch.
These are the measures destined for her soul.

III

Jove in the clouds had his inhuman birth.
No mother suckled him, no sweet land gave
Large-mannered motions to his mythy mind.
He moved among us, as a muttering king,
Magnificent, would move among his hinds,
Until our blood, commingling, virginal,
With heaven, brought such requital to desire
The very hinds discerned it, in a star.
Shall our blood fail? Or shall it come to be
The blood of paradise? And shall the earth
Seem all of paradise that we shall know?
The sky will be much friendlier then than now,
A part of labour and a part of pain,
And next in glory to enduring love,
Not this dividing and indifferent blue.

IV

She says, 'I am content when wakened birds,
Before they fly, test the reality
Of misty fields, by their sweet questionings;
But when the birds are gone, and their warm fields
Return no more, where, then, is paradise?'

There is not any haunt of prophecy,
Nor any old chimera of the grave,
Neither the golden underground, nor isle
Melodious, where spirits gat them home,
Nor visionary south, nor cloudy palm
Remote on heaven's hill, that has endured
As April's green endures; or will endure
Like her remembrance of awakened birds,
Or her desire for June and evening, tipped
By the consummation of the swallow's wings.

V

She says, 'But in contentment I still feel
The need of some imperishable bliss.'
Death is the mother of beauty; hence from her,
Alone, shall come fulfilment to our dreams
And our desires. Although she strews the leaves
Of sure obliteration on our paths,
The path sick sorrow took, the many paths
Where triumph rang its brassy phrase, or love
Whispered a little out of tenderness,
She makes the willow shiver in the sun
For maidens who were wont to sit and gaze
Upon the grass, relinquished to their feet.
She causes boys to pile new plums and pears
On disregarded plate. The maidens taste
And stray impassioned in the littering leaves.

VI

Is there no change of death in paradise?
Does ripe fruit never fall? Or do the boughs
Hang always heavy in that perfect sky,
Unchanging, yet so like our perishing earth,
With rivers like our own that seek for seas
They never find, the same receding shores
That never touch with inarticulate pang?

Why set the pear upon those river-banks
Or spice the shores with odours of the plum?
Alas, that they should wear our colours there,
The silken weavings of our afternoons,
And pick the strings of our insipid lutes!
Death is the mother of beauty, mystical,
Within whose burning bosom we devise
Our earthly mothers waiting, sleeplessly.

VII

Supple and turbulent, a ring of men
Shall chant in orgy on a summer morn
Their boisterous devotion to the sun,
Not as a god, but as a god might be,
Naked among them, like a savage source.
Their chant shall be a chant of paradise,
Out of their blood, returning to the sky;
And in their chant shall enter, voice by voice,
The windy lake wherein their lord delights,
The trees, like serafim, and echoing hills,
That choir among themselves long afterward.
They shall know well the heavenly fellowship
Of men that perish and of summer morn.
And whence they came and whither they shall go.
The dew upon their feet shall manifest.

VIII

She hears, upon that water without sound,
A voice that cries, 'The tomb in Palestine
Is not the porch of spirits lingering.
It is the grave of Jesus, where he lay.'
We live in an old chaos of the sun,
Or old dependency of day and night,
Or island solitude, unsponsored, free,
Of that wide water, inescapable.
Deer walk upon our mountains, and the quail

Whistle about us their spontaneous cries;
Sweet berries ripen in the wilderness;
And, in the isolation of the sky,
At evening, casual flocks of pigeons make
Ambiguous undulations as they sink,
Downward to darkness, on extended wings.

DRY LOAF

It is equal to living in a tragic land
To live in a tragic time.
Regard now the sloping, mountainous rocks
And the river that batters its way over stones,
Regard the hovels of those that live in this land.

That was what I painted behind the loaf,
The rocks not even touched by snow,
The pines along the river and the dry men blown
Brown as the bread, thinking of birds
Flying from burning countries and brown sand shores,

Birds that came like dirty water in waves
Flowing above the rocks, flowing over the sky,
As if the sky was a current that bore them along,
Spreading them as waves spread flat on the shore,
One after another washing the mountains bare.

It was the battering of drums I heard
It was hunger, it was the hungry that cried
And the waves, the waves were soldiers moving,
Marching and marching in a tragic time
Below me, on the asphalt, under the trees.

It was soldiers went marching over the rocks
And still the birds came, came in watery flocks,
Because it was spring and the birds had to come.
No doubt that soldiers had to be marching
And that drums had to be rolling, rolling, rolling.

WOMAN LOOKING AT A VASE OF FLOWERS

It was as if thunder took form upon
The piano, that time: the time when the crude
And jealous grandeurs of sun and sky
Scattered themselves in the garden, like
The wind dissolving into birds
The clouds becoming braided girls.
It was like the sea poured out again
In east wind beating the shutters at night.

Hoot,   little owl within her,   how
High blue became particular
In the leaf and bud and how the red,
Flicked into pieces, points of air,
Became—how the central, essential red
Escaped its large abstraction, became,
First, summer, then a lesser time,
Then the sides of peaches, of dusky pears.

Hoot how the inhuman colours fell
Into place beside her, where she was,
Like human conciliations, more like
A profounder reconciling, an act,
An affirmation free from doubt.
The crude and jealous formlessness
Became the form and the fragrance of things
Without clairvoyance, close to her.

BETHOU ME, SAID SPARROW

Bethou me, said sparrow, to the crackled blade,
And you, and you, bethou me as you blow,
When in my coppice you behold me be.

Ah, ké! the bloody wren, the felon jay,
Ké-ké, the jug-throated robin pouring out,
Bethou, bethou, bethou me in my glade.

There was such idiot minstrelsy in rain,
So many clappers going without bells,
That these bethous compose a heavenly gong.

One voice repeating, one tireless chorister,
The phrases of a single phrase, ké-ké,
A single text, granite monotony,

One sole face, like a photograph of fate,
Glass-blower's destiny, bloodless episcopus,
Eye without lid, mind without any dream—

These are of minstrels lacking minstrelsy,
Of an earth in which the first leaf is the tale
Of leaves, in which the sparrow is a bird

Of stone, that never changes. Bethou him, you
And you, bethou him and bethou. It is
A sound like any other. It will end.
(from *Notes toward a Supreme Fiction*)

WE REASON OF THESE THINGS

We reason of these things with later reason
And we make of what we see, what we see clearly
And have seen, a place dependent on ourselves.

There was a mystic marriage in Catawba,
At noon it was on the mid-day of the year
Between a great captain and the maiden Bawda.

This was their ceremonial hymn: Anon
We loved but would no marriage make. Anon
The one refused the other one to take,

Foreswore the sipping of the marriage wine.
Each must the other take not for his high,
His puissant front nor for her subtle sound,

The shoo-shoo-shoo of secret cymbals round.
Each must the other take as sign, short sign
To stop the whirlwind, balk the elements.

The great captain loved the ever-hill Catawba
And therefore married Bawda, whom he found there,
And Bawda loved the captain as she loved the sun.

They married well because the marriage-place
Was what they loved. It was neither heaven nor hell.
They were love's characters come face to face.

(from Notes toward a Supreme Fiction)

WALLACE
STEVENS

Witter Bynner

(1881-   )

JEREMIAH

Roses have been his bed so long that he
Constructs a mat of thorns for lying on;
People have flattered him, until the sea
Becomes a preferable monotone.
He sets his masonry upon the brink
Of lamentation, out of his window peers
Toward waves that ever rise only to sink
Confused and lost as he among his years.
A ship alive becomes to him a hull
Charred and undone, the fumble of a wreck;
His dreams are but the droppings of a gull
Caught in a noose of seaweed round his neck;
And crying like a maniac toward the sky,
He pulls mankind in after him, to die.

William Carlos Williams

(1883-   )

SUNDAY IN THE PARK

And still the picnickers come on, now
early afternoon, and scatter through the
trees over the fenced-in acres   .

                         Voices!
multiple and inarticulate   .   voices
clattering loudly to the sun, to
the clouds. Voices!
assaulting the air gaily from all sides.

—among which the ear strains to catch
the movement of one voice among the rest
—a reed-like voice
                     of peculiar accent

Thus she finds what peace there is, reclines,
before his approach, stroked
by their clambering feet—for pleasure

                It is all for
pleasure   .   their feet   .   aimlessly
        wandering

The 'great beast' come to sun himself
                     as he may
.   .   their dreams mingling,
aloof

Let us be reasonable!

WILLIAM
CARLOS
WILLIAMS
Sunday in the park,
limited by the escarpment, eastward; to
the west abutting on the old road: recreation
with a view! the binoculars chained
to anchored stanchions along the east wall—
beyond which, a hawk

soars!

—a trumpet sounds fitfully.

Stand at the rampart (use a metronome
if your ear is deficient, one made in Hungary
if you prefer)
and look away north by east where the church
spires still spend their wits against
the sky   .   to the ball-park
in the hollow with its minute figures running
—beyond the gap where the river
plunges into the narrow gorge, unseen

—and the imagination soars, as a voice
beckons, a thundrous voice, endless
—as sleep: the voice
that has ineluctably called them—

that unmoving roar!
churches and factories
(at a price)
together, summoned them from the pit   .

—his voice, one among many (unheard)
moving under all.

The mountain quivers.

Time! Count! Sever and mark time!

So during the early afternoon, from place
to place he moves,
his voice mingling with other voices
—the voice in his voice
opening his old throat, blowing out his lips,
kindling his mind (more
than his mind will kindle)

                    —following the hikers.

At last he comes to the idlers' favourite
haunts, the picturesque summit, where
the blue-stone (rust-red where exposed)
has been faulted at various levels
                (ferns rife among the stones)
into rough terraces and partly closed in
dens of sweet grass, the ground gently sloping.

loiterers in groups straggle
over the bare rock-table—scratched by their
boot-nails more than the glacier scratched
them—walking indifferent through
each other's privacy

                    —in any case
the centre of movement, the core of gaiety.

here a young man, perhaps sixteen,
is sitting with his back to the rock among
some ferns playing a guitar, dead pan

The rest are eating and drinking.

                    The big guy
in the black hat is too full to move

                        but Mary
is up!

WILLIAM
CARLOS
WILLIAMS

81

Come on! Wassa ma'? You got
broken leg?

It is this air!
the air of the Midi
and the old cultures intoxicates them:
present!

—lifts one arm holding the cymbals
of her thoughts, cocks her old head
and dances! raising her skirts:

La la la la!

What a bunch of bums! Afraid somebody see
you?
Blah!
Excrementi!
—she spits.
Look a' me, Grandma! Everybody too damn
lazy.

This is the old, the very old, old upon old,
the undying: even to the minute gestures,
the hand holding the cup, the wine
spilling, the arm stained by it:
Remember

the peon in the lost
Eisenstein film drinking

from a wine-skin with the abandon
of a horse drinking

so that it slopped down his chin?
down his neck, dribbling

over his shirt-front and down
onto his pants—laughing, toothless?

Heavenly man!

—the leg raised, verisimilitude
even to the coarse contours of the leg, the
bovine touch! The leer, the cave of it,
the female of it facing the male, the satyr—
    (Priapus!)
with that lonely implication, goatherd
and goat, fertility, the attack, drunk,
cleansed   .

                Rejected. Even the film
suppressed   :   but   .   persistent

The picnickers laugh on the rocks celebrating
the varied Sunday of their loves with
its declining light—

Walking—

look down (from a ledge) into this grassy
den
        (somewhat removed from the traffic)
                        above whose brows
a moon! where she lies sweating at his side:

                    She stirs, distraught,
against him—wounded (drunk), moves
against him (a lump) desiring,
against him, bored   .
flagrantly bored and sleeping, a
beer bottle still grasped spear-like
in his hand   .

while the small, sleepless boys, who
have climbed the columnar rocks

83

overhanging the pair (where they lie
overt upon the grass, besieged—

careless in their narrow cell under
the crowd's feet) stare down,
                                                    from history!
at them, puzzled and in the sexless
light (of childhood) bored equally,
go charging off   .

                        There where
the movement throbs openly
and you can hear the Evangelist shouting!

                                        —moving nearer
            she—lean as a goat—leans
            her lean belly to the man's backside
            toying with the clips of his
            suspenders   .

—to which he adds his useless voice:
until there moves in his sleep
a music that is whole, inequivocal (in
his sleep, sweating in his sleep—labouring
against sleep, agasp!)
                        —and does not waken.

Sees, alive (asleep)
                        —the fall's roar entering
his sleep (to be fulfilled)
                                                reborn
in his sleep—scattered over the mountain
severally

            —by which he woos here, severally.

And the amnesic crowd (the scattered),
called about strains
to catch the movement of one voice

                                        hears
            Pleasure! Pleasure!

                                        —feels
half dismayed, the afternoon of complex
voices its own—
                and is relieved
                        (relived)
        A cop is directing traffic
        across the main road up
        a little wooded slope toward
        the conveniences:
                        oaks, choke-cherry,
dogwoods, white and green, iron-wood;
humped roots matted into the shallow soil
—mostly gone: rock out-croppings
polished by the feet of the picnickers:
sweetbarked sassafras

leaning from the rancid grease:
                        deformity—
—to be deciphered (a horn, a trumpet!)
an elucidation by multiplicity,
a corrosion, a parasitic curd, a clarion
for belief, to be good dogs   :

NO DOGS ALLOWED AT LARGE IN THIS PARK
                        (from *PATERSON*)

WILLIAM
CARLOS
WILLIAMS

TO DAPHNE AND VIRGINIA

THE SMELL OF the heat is boxwood
   when rousing us
     a movement of the air
stirs our thoughts
   that had no life in them
     to a life, a life in which
two women agonize:
   to live and to breathe is no less.
     Two young women.
The box odour
   is the odour of that of which
     partaking separately,
each to herself
   I partake also

    . .   separately.

BE PATIENT THAT I address you in a poem,
   there is no other
     fit medium.
The mind
   lives there. It is uncertain,
     can trick and leave us
agonized. But for resources
   what can equal it?
     There is nothing. We
should be lost
   without its wings to
     fly off upon.

THE MIND IS the cause of our distresses
   but of it we can build anew.
     Oh something more than
it flies off to:
   a woman's world,
     of crossed sticks, stopping
thought. A new world
   is only a new mind.

And the mind and the poem
are all apiece.
Two young women
to be snared,
odour of box,
to bind and hold them
for the mind labours.

ALL WOMEN ARE fated similarly
facing men
and there is always
another, such as I,
who loves them,
loves all women, but
finds himself, touching them,
like other men,
often confused.

I HAVE TWO sons,
the husbands of these women,
who live also
in a world of love,
apart.
Shall this odour of box in
the heat
not also touch them
fronting a world of women
from which they are
debarred
by the very scents which draw them on
against easy access?

IN OUR FAMILY we stammer unless,
half mad,
we come to speech at last

AND I AM not
a young man.

My love encumbers me.
It is a love
less than
a young man's love but,
like this box odour
more penetrant, infinitely
more penetrant,
in that sense not to be resisted.

THERE IS, IN the hard
give and take
of a man's life with
a woman
a thing which is not the stress itself
but beyond
and above
that,
something that wants to rise
and shake itself
free. We are not chickadees
on a bare limb
with a worm in the mouth.
The worm is in our brains
and concerns them
and not food for our
offspring, wants to disrupt
our thought
and throw it
to the newspapers
or anywhere.
There is, in short,
a counter stress,
born of the sexual shock,
which survives it
consonant with the moon,
to keep its own mind.

There is, of course
more.
Women
are not alone
in that. At least
while this healing odour is abroad
one can write a poem.

STAYING HERE in the country
on an old farm
we eat our breakfasts
on a balcony under an elm.
The shrubs below us
are neglected. And
there, penned in,
or he would eat the garden,
lives a pet goose who
tilts his head
sidewise
and looks up at us,
a very quiet old fellow
who writes no poems.
Fine mornings we sit there
while birds
come and go.
A pair of robins
is building a nest
for the second time
this season. Men
against their reason
speak of love, sometimes,
when they are old. It is
all they can do
or watch a heavy goose
who waddles, slopping
noisily in the mud of
his pool.

Elinor Wylie

(1885-1928)

LAVISH KINDNESS

Indulgent giants burned to crisp
The oak-trees of a dozen shires
Adorning thus a will-o'-the-wisp
With momentary pomp of fires.

The waters of an inland sea
Were magicked to a mountain peak
Enabling dwindled pools to be
Cool to a single swallow's beak.

But whether prodigies of waste,
Or idle, or beneficent,
Such deeds are not performed in haste
And none has fathomed their intent.

DOOMSDAY

The end of everything approaches;
I hear it coming
Loud as the wheels of painted coaches
On turnpikes drumming;
Loud as the pomp of plumy hearses,
Or pennoned charges;
Loud as when every oar reverses
Venetian barges;
Loud as the caves of covered bridges
Fulfilled with rumble

Of hooves; and loud as cloudy ridges
When glaciers tumble;
Like creeping thunder this continues
Diffused and distant,
Loud in our ears and in our sinews,
Insane, insistent;
Loud as a lion scorning carrion
Further and further;
Loud as the ultimate loud clarion
Or the first murther.

SHEPHERD'S HOLIDAY

Too honest for a gypsy, too lazy for a farmer,
What should you be but a shepherd on the hills,
Herding sheep with sad faces
Over grass-grown places,
High above a web of streams and willow-trees and mills?

Too tame for a gypsy, too wild for a dairy-maid,
What could I be but a silly goose-girl,
Tending hissing white snakes
By weed-green lakes,
Crying in the dew-fall with my hair out of curl?

Too silent for the neighbours, too simple for the towns-
people,
What shall we do who love each other so?
I'll teach your grey sheep
To guard you from the steep,
You'll catch me back from drowning where my dark lake
lies deep,
I'll pluck a feather pillow that shall sing you to sleep
Up among the rocks where the blueberries grow.

FULL MOON

My bands of silk and miniver
Momently grew heavier;
The black gauze was beggarly thin;
The ermine muffled mouth and chin;
I could not suck the moonlight in.

Harlequin in lozenges
Of love and hate, I walked in these
Striped and ragged rigmaroles;
Along the pavement my footsoles
Trod warily on living coals.

Shouldering the thoughts I loathed,
In their corrupt disguises clothed,
Mortality I could not tear
From my ribs, to leave them bare
Ivory in silver air.

There I walked, and there I raged;
The spiritual savage caged
Within my skeleton, raged afresh
To feel, behind a carnal mesh,
The clean bones crying in the flesh.

Ezra Pound

(1885-   )

THE LAKE ISLE

O God, O Venus, O Mercury, patron of thieves,
Give me in due time, I beseech you, a little tobacco-shop,
With the little bright boxes
      piled up neatly upon the shelves
And the loose fragrant cavendish
      and the shag,
And the bright Virginia
      loose under the bright glass cases,
And a pair of scales not too greasy,
And the whores dropping in for a word or two in
      passing,
For a flip word, and to tidy their hair a bit.

O God, O Venus, O Mercury, patron of thieves,
Lend me a little tobacco-shop,
      or install me in any profession
Save this damn'd profession of writing,
      where one needs one's brains all the time.

PROVINCIA DESERTA

At Rochecoart,
Where the hills part
      in three ways,
And three valleys, full of winding roads,
Fork out to south and north,
There is a place of trees . . . grey with lichen.

I have walked there
                        thinking of old days.
At Chalais
                        is a pleached arbour;
Old pensioners and old protected women
Have the right there—
                        it is charity.
I have crept over old rafters,
                        peering down
Over the Dronne,
                        over a stream full of lilies.
Eastward the road lies,
                        Aubeterre is eastward,
With a garrulous old man at the inn.
I know the roads in that place:
Mareuil to the north-east,
                        La Tour,
There are three keeps near Mareuil,
And an old woman,
                        glad to hear Arnaut,
Glad to lend one dry clothing.

I have walked
                        into Perigord,
I have seen the torch-flames, high-leaping,
Painting the front of that church;
Heard, under the dark, whirling laughter.
I have looked back over the stream
                        and seen the high building,
Seen the long minarets, the white shafts.
I have gone in Ribeyrac
                        and in Sarlat,
I have climbed rickety stairs, heard talk of Croy,
Walked over En Bertran's old layout,
Have seen Narbonne, and Cahors and Chalus,
Have seen Excideuil, carefully fashioned.

I have said:
       'Here such a one walked.
'Here Cœur-de-Lion was slain.
       'Here was good singing.
'Here one man hastened his step.
       'Here one lay panting.'
I have looked south from Hautefort,
       thinking of Montaignac, southward.
I have lain in Rocafixada,
       level with sunset,
Have seen the copper come down
       tingeing the mountains,
I have seen the fields, pale, clear as an emerald,
Sharp peaks, high spurs, distant castles.
I have said: 'The old roads have lain here.
'Men have gone by such and such valleys
'Where the great halls were closer together.'
I have seen Foix on its rock, seen Toulouse, and
       Arles greatly altered,
I have seen the ruined 'Dorata.'
       I have said:
'Riquier! Guido.'
       I have thought of the second Troy,
Some little prized place in Auvergnat:
Two men tossing a coin, one keeping a castle,
One set on the highway to sing.
       He sang a woman.
Auvergne rose to the song;
       The Dauphin backed him.
'The castle to Austors!'
       'Pieire kept the singing—
A fair man and a pleasant.'
       He won the lady,
Stole her away for himself, kept her against armed
       force:
So ends that story.
That age is gone;

Pieire de Maensac is gone
I have walked over these roads;
I have thought of them living.

SOUTH-FOLK IN COLD COUNTRY

The Dai horse neighs against the bleak wind of Etsu,
The birds of Etsu have no love for En, in the North,
Emotion is born out of habit.
Yesterday we went out of the Wild-Goose gate,
To-day from the Dragon-Pen.[1]
Surprised. Desert turmoil. Sea sun.
Flying snow bewilders the barbarian heaven.
Lice swarm like ants over our accoutrements.
Mind and spirit drive on the feathery banners.
Hard fight gets no reward.
Loyalty is hard to explain.
Who will be sorry for General Rishogu,
                    the swift moving,
Whose white head is lost for this province?

HOMAGE TO SEXTUS PROPERTIUS, PART V

I

Now if ever it is time to cleanse Helicon;
                    to lead Emathian horses afield,
And to name over the census of my chiefs in the Roman
        camp.
If I have not the faculty, 'The bare attempt would be praise-
        worthy.'
'In things of similar magnitude
                    the mere will to act is sufficient.'

---

[1] i.e., we have been warring from one end of the empire to the other,
now east, now west, on each border.

The primitive ages sang Venus,

      the last sings of a tumult,
And I also will sing war when this matter of a girl is
  exhausted.
I with my beak hauled ashore would proceed in a more
  stately manner,
My Muse is eager to instruct me in a new gamut, or
  gambetto,
Up, up my soul, from your lowly cantilation,
       put on a timely vigour.
Oh august Pierides! Now for a large-mouthed product.
Thus:
'The Euphrates denies its protection to the Parthian and
      apologizes for Crassus,'
And 'It is, I think, India which now gives necks to your
  triumph,'
And so forth, Augustus. 'Virgin Arabia shakes in her inmost
  dwelling.'
If any land shrink into a distant seacoast,
    it is a mere postponement of your domination.
And I shall follow the camp, I shall be duly celebrated for
    singing the affairs of your cavalry.
May the fates watch over my day.

II

Yet you ask on what account I write so many love-lyrics
And whence this soft book comes into my mouth.
Neither Calliope nor Apollo sung these things into my ear,
  My genius is no more than a girl.

If she with ivory fingers drive a tune through the lyre,
  We look at the process.
How easy the moving fingers; if hair is mussed on her
  forehead,
If she goes in a gleam of Cos, in a slither of dyed stuff,
There is a volume in the matter; if her eyelids sink into sleep,

There are new jobs for the author;
And if she plays with me with her shirt off,
    We shall construct many Iliads.
And whatever she does or says
    We shall spin long yarns out of nothing.

Thus much the fates have allotted me, and if, Maecenas,
I were able to lead heroes into armour, I would not,
Neither would I warble of Titans, nor of Ossa
                         spiked onto Olympus,
Nor of causeways over Pelion,
Nor of Thebes in its ancient respectability,
            nor of Homer's reputation in Pergamus,
Nor of Xerxes' two-barreled kingdom, nor of Remus and
    his royal family,
Nor of dignified Carthaginian characters,
Nor of Welsh mines and the profit Marus had out of them.
I should remember Caesar's affairs . . . for a background,
Although Callimachus did without them,
                     and without Theseus,
Without an inferno, without Achilles attended of gods,
Without Ixion, and without the sons of Menoetius
    and the Argo and without Jove's grave and the Titans.

And my ventricles do not palpitate to Caesarial *ore rotundos*,
Nor to the tune of the Phrygian fathers.
Sailor, of winds; a ploughman, concerning his oxen;
Soldier, the enumeration of wounds; the sheep-feeder of
    ewes;
We, in our narrow bed, turning aside from battles:
Each man where he can, wearing out the day in his manner.

III

It is noble to die of love, and honourable to remain un-
                    cuckolded for a season.
And she speaks ill of light women,
                and will not praise Homer
Because Helen's conduct is 'unsuitable'.

E. P. ODE POUR L'ELECTION
DE SON SEPULCHRE

EZRA
POUND

For three years, out of key with his time,
He strove to resuscitate the dead art
Of poetry; to maintain 'the sublime'
In the old sense. Wrong from the start—

No, hardly, but seeing he had been born
In a half-savage country, out of date;
Bent resolutely on wringing lilies from the acorn;
Capaneus; trout for factitious bait;

Ἴδμεν γάρ τοι πάνθ', ὅσ' ἐνὶ Τροίη
Caught in the unstopped ear;
Giving the rocks small lee-way
The chopped seas held him, therefore, that year.

His true Penelope was Flaubert,
He fished by obstinate isles;
Observed the elegance of Circe's hair
Rather than the mottoes on sundials.

Unaffected by 'the march of events',
He passed from men's memory in *l'an trentiesme*,
De son eage; the case presents
No adjunct to the Muses' diadem.

CANTO XLVII

Who even dead, yet hath his mind entire!
This sound came in the dark
First must thou go the road
          to hell
And to the bower of Ceres' daughter Proserpine,
Through overhanging dark, to see Tiresias,

Eyeless that was, a shade, that is in hell
So full of knowing that the beefy men know less than he,
Ere thou come to thy road's end.
                            Knowledge the shade of a shade,
Yet must thou sail after knowledge
Knowing less than drugged beasts. *phtheggometha
thasson*

φθεγγώμεθα θᾶσσον
            The small lamps drift in the bay
And the sea's claw gathers them.
Neptunus drinks after neap-tide.
Tamuz! Tamuz!!
The red flame going seaward.
            By this gate art thou measured.
From the long boats they have set lights in the water,
The sea's claw gathers them outward.
Scilla's dogs snarl at the cliff's base,
The white teeth gnaw in under the crag,
But in the pale night the small lamps float seaward

                            τυ Διώνα
                            TU DIONA

και Μοῖρα τ'"Αδονιν
KAI MOIRA T' ADONIN

The sea is streaked red with Adonis,
The lights flicker red in small jars.
Wheat shoots rise new by the altar,
            flower from the swift seed.
Two span, two span to a woman,
Beyond that she believes not. Nothing is of any importance.
To that is she bent, her intention,
To that art thou called ever turning intention,
Whether by night the owl-call, whether by sap in shoot,
Never idle, by no means by no wiles intermittent
Moth is called over mountain
The bull runs blind on the sword, *naturans*

To the cave art thou called, Odysseus,
By Molü hast thou respite for a little,
By Molü art thou freed from the one bed
       that thou may'st return to another
The stars are not in her counting,
       To her they are but wandering holes.
Begin thy ploughing
When the Pleiades go down to their rest,
Begin thy ploughing
40 days are they under seaboard,
Thus do in fields by seaboard
And in valleys winding down toward the sea.
When the cranes fly high
       think of ploughing.
By this gate art thou measured
Thy day is between a door and a door
Two oxen are yoked for ploughing
Or six in the hill field
White bulk under olives, a score for drawing down stone,
Here the mules are gabled with slate on the hill road.
Thus was it in time.
And the small stars now fall from the olive branch,
Forked shadow falls dark on the terrace
More black than the floating martin
       that has no care for your presence,
His wing-print is black on the roof tiles
And the print is gone with his cry.
So light is thy weight on Tellus
Thy notch no deeper indented
Thy weight less than the shadow
Yet hast thou gnawed through the mountain,
       Scilla's white teeth less sharp.
Hast thou found a nest softer than cunnus
Or hast thou found better rest
Hast'ou a deeper planting, doth thy death year
Bring swifter shoot?
Hast thou entered more deeply the mountain?

EZRA The light has entered the cave. Io! Io!
POUND The light has gone down into the cave,
Splendour on splendour!
By prong have I entered these hills:
That the grass grow from my body,
That I hear the roots speaking together,
The air is new on my leaf,
The forked boughs shake with the wind.
Is Zephyrus more light on the bough, Apeliota
more light on the almond branch?
By this door have I entered the hill.
Falleth,
Adonis falleth.
Fruit cometh after. The small lights drift out with the tide,
sea's claw has gathered them outward,
Four banners to every flower
The sea's claw draws the lamps outward.
Think thus of thy ploughing
When the seven stars go down to their rest
Forty days for their rest, by seaboard
And in valleys that wind down toward the sea

και Μοῖρα τ'"Αδονιν

KAI MOIRA T' ADONIN

When the almond bough puts forth its flame,
When the new shoots are brought to the altar,

τυ Διῳνα, και Μοῖρα

TU DIONA, KAI MOIRA

και Μοῖρα τ'"Αδονιν

KAI MOIRA T' ADONIN

    that hath the gift of healing,
that hath the power over wild beasts.

Louis Untermeyer

(1885-   )

SONG TOURNEMENT: NEW STYLE

Rain, said the first, as it falls in Venice
Is like the dropping of golden pennies
Into a sea as smooth and bright
As a bowl of curdled malachite.

Storm, sang the next, in the streets of Peking
Is like the ghost of a yellow sea-king,
Scooping the dust to find if he may
Discover what earth has hidden away.

The rush of Spring, smiled the third, in Florence
Is wave upon wave of laughing torrents,
A flood of birds, a water-voiced calling,
A green rain rising instead of falling.

The wind, cried the fourth, in the bay of Naples
Is a quarrel of leaves among the maples,
A war of sunbeams idly fanned,
A whisper softer than sand on sand.

Then spoke the last: God's endless tears,
Too great for Heaven, anoint the spheres,
While every drop becomes a well
In the fathomless, thirsty heart of Hell.

And these five bards, who could boast of travel
Fifty miles from their native gravel,
Rose in the sunlight and offered their stanzas
At the shrine of the Poetry Contest in Kansas.

John Gould Fletcher

(1886-1946)

IV. THE WINDMILLS

The windmills, like great sunflowers of steel,
Lift themselves proudly over the straggling houses;
And at their feet the deep blue-green alfalfa
Cuts the desert like the stroke of a sword.

Yellow melon flowers
Crawl beneath the withered peach-trees;
A date-palm throws its heavy fronds of steel
Against the scoured metallic sky.

The houses, double-roofed for coolness,
Cower amid the manzanita scrub.
A man with jingling spurs
Walks heavily out of a vine-bowered doorway,
Mounts his pony, rides away.

The windmills stare at the sun.
The yellow earth cracks and blisters.
Everything is still.

In the afternoon
The wind takes dry waves of heat and tosses them,
Mingled with dust, up and down the streets,
Against the belfry with its green bells:

And, after sunset, when the sky
Becomes a green and orange fan,
The windmills, like great sunflowers on dried stalks,
Stare hard at the sun they cannot follow.

Turning, turning, forever turning   JOHN
In the chill night-wind that sweeps over the valley,   GOULD
With the shriek and the clank of the pumps groaning FLETCHER
    beneath them,
And the choking gurgle of tepid water.

H.D.

(1886-   )

AN INCIDENT HERE AND THERE

An incident here and there,
and rails gone (for guns)
from your (and my) old town square:

mists and mist-grey, no colour,
still the Luxor bee, chick and hare
pursue unalterable purpose

in green, rose-red, lapis;
they continue to prophesy
from the stone papyrus:

there, as here, ruin opens
the tomb, the temple; enter,
there as here, there are no doors:

the shrine lies open to the sky,
the rain falls, here, there
sand drifts; eternity endures:

ruin everywhere, yet as the fallen roof
leaves the sealed room
open to the air,

so, through our desolation,
thoughts stir, inspiration stalks us
through gloom:

unaware, spirit announces the Presence; H.D.
shivering overtakes us,
as of old, Samuel:

trembling at a known street-corner,
we know not nor are known;
the Pythian pronounces—we pass on

to another cellar, to another sliced wall
where poor utensils show
like rare objects in a museum;

Pompeii has nothing to teach us,
we know crack of volcanic fissure,
slow flow of terrible lava,

pressure on heart, lungs, the brain
about to burst its brittle case
(what the skull can endure!):

over us, Apocryphal fire,
under us, the earth sway, dip of a floor,
slope of a pavement

where men roll, drunk
with a new bewilderment,
sorcery, bedevilment:

the bone-frame was made for
no such shock knit within terror,
yet the skeleton stood up to it:

the flesh? it was melted away,
the heart burnt out, dead ember,
tendons, muscles shattered, outer husk dismembered,

yet the frame held:
we passed the flame: we wonder
what saved us? what for?

AH (YOU SAY), THIS IS HOLY WISDOM

I

Ah (you say), this is Holy Wisdom,
Sancta Sophia, the SS of the *Sanctus Spiritus*,

so by facile reasoning, logically
the incarnate symbol of the Holy Ghost;

your Holy Ghost was an apple-tree
smouldering—or rather now burgeoning

with flowers; the fruit of the Tree?
this is the new Eve who comes

clearly to return, to retrieve
what she has lost the race,

given over to sin, to death;
she brings the Book of Life, obviously.

II

This is a symbol of beauty (you continue),
she is Our Lady universally,

I see her as you project her,
not out of place

flanked by Corinthian capitals,
or in a Coptic nave,

or frozen above the centre door
of a Gothic cathedral;

you have done very well by her
(to repeat your own phrase),

you have carved her tall and unmistakable,
a hieratic figure, the veiled Goddess,

whether of the seven delights,
whether of the seven spear-points.

III

O yes—you understand, I say,
this is all most satisfactory,

but she wasn't hieratic, she wasn't frozen,
she wasn't very tall;

she is the Vestal
from the days of Numa,

she carries over the cult
of the *Bona Dea*,

she carries a book but it is not
the tome of the ancient wisdom,

the pages, I imagine, are the blank pages
of the unwritten volume of the new;

all you say, is implicit,
all that and much more;

but she is not shut up in a cave
like a Sibyl; she is not

imprisoned in leaden bars
in a coloured window;

she is Psyche, the butterfly,
out of the cocoon.

IV

But nearer than Guardian Angel
or good Daemon,

she is the counter-coin-side
of primitive terror;

she is not-fear, she is not-war,
but she is no symbolic figure

of peace, charity, chastity, goodness,
faith, hope, reward;

she is not Justice with eyes
blindfolded like Love's;

I grant you the dove's symbolic purity,
I grant you her face was innocent

and immaculate and her veils
like the Lamb's Bride,

but the Lamb was not with her,
either as Bridegroom or Child;

her attention is undivided,
we are her bridegroom and lamb;

her book is our book; written
or unwritten, its pages will reveal

a tale of a Fisherman,
a tale of a jar or jars,

the same—different—the same attributes,
different yet the same as before.

John Hall Wheelock

(1886-   )

THE YEARS

My dreams wear thinner as the years go by:
    The stony face of Fate, into my own,
Stares, with that granite look of hers—and I
    Stare back, with a still face, but not of stone.

RECONCILIATION

At the foot of a great pine, in the wild country
Westward, well inland, we uncovered them,
The skeletons of a fish-hawk and a fish,
Half-buried in dead leaves. The long pursuit,
And the flight, ended; the terror, the conquest, ended,
And the wars that divide Being, they rested there—
Emblems of the inexplicable will.

Robinson Jeffers

(1887-   )

SUMMER HOLIDAY

When the sun shouts and people abound
One thinks there were the ages of stone and the age of bronze
And the iron age; iron the unstable metal;
Steel made of iron, unstable as his mother; the towered-up
   cities
Will be stains of rust on mounds of plaster.
Roots will not pierce the heaps for a time, kind rains will
   cure them,
Then nothing will remain of the iron age
And all these people but a thigh-bone or so, a poem
Stuck in the world's thought, splinters of glass
In the rubbish dumps, a concrete dam far off in the
   mountain. . . .

I. REFERENCE TO A PASSAGE IN PLUTARCH'S LIFE OF SULLA

The people buying and selling, consuming pleasures, talking
   in the archways,
Were all suddenly struck quiet
And ran from under stone to look up at the sky: so shrill and
   mournful,
So fierce and final, a brazen
Pealing of trumpets high up in the air, in the summer blue
   over Tuscany.
They marvelled; the soothsayers answered:
'Although the Gods are little troubled toward men, at the
   end of each period

A sign is declared in heaven
Indicating new times, new customs, a changed people; the
    Romans
Rule, and Etruria is finished;
A wise mariner will trim the sails to the wind.'
                         I heard yesterday
So shrill and mournful a trumpet-blast,
It was hard to be wise. . . . You must eat change and endure;
    not be much troubled
For the people; they will have their happiness.
When the republic grows too heavy to endure, then Caesar
    will carry it;
When life grows hateful, there's power . . .

NOVEMBER SURF

Some lucky day each November great waves awake and are
    drawn
Like smoking mountains bright from the west
And come and cover the cliff with white violent cleanness:
    then suddenly
The old granite forgets half a year's filth:
The orange-peel, eggshells, papers, pieces of clothing, the
    clots
Of dung in corners of the rock, and used
Sheaths that make light love safe in the evenings: all the
    droppings of the summer
Idlers washed off in a winter ecstasy:
I think this cumbered continent envies its cliff then . . .
    But all seasons
The earth, in her childlike prophetic sleep,
Keeps dreaming of the bath of a storm that prepares up the
    long coast
Of the future to scour more than her sea-lines:
The cities gone down, the people fewer and the hawks more
    numerous,

The rivers mouth to source pure; when the two-footed
Mammal, being someways one of the nobler animals,
   regains
The dignity of room, the value of rareness.

I SHALL LAUGH PURELY

I

Turn from that girl
Your fixed blue eyes.
Boy-slender she is,
And a face as beautiful as a hawk's face.
History passes like falling rocks.

I am old as a stone,
But she is beautiful.
War is coming.
All the fine boys will go off to war.
History passes like falling rocks.

Oh, that one's to marry
Another old man;
You won't be helped
When your tall sons go away to war.
History falls on your head like rocks.

Keep a straight mind
In the evil time
In the mad-dog time
Why may not an old man run mad?
History falls like rocks in the dark,
All will be worse confounded soon.

II

Count the glories of this time,
Count that girl's beauty, then count England,
Bleeding, at bay, magnificent,
At last a lion,
For all will be worse confounded soon.

Count that girl's beauty, count the coast-range,
The steep rock that stops the Pacific,
Count the surf on its precipice,
the hawks in its air,
For all will be worse confounded soon.

Count its eagles and wild boars,
Count the great blue-black winter storms,
Heavy rain and the hurricane,
Get them by heart,
For all will be worse confounded soon.

Count no human thing but only
England's great fight and that girl's beauty,
History passes like falling
Rocks in the dark,
And all will be worse confounded soon.

III

But this, I steadily assure you, is not the world's end,
Nor even the end of a civilization. It is not so late as you
    think: give nature time.
These wars will end, and I shall lead a troupe of shaky old
    men through Europe and America,
Old drunkards, worn-out lechers; fallen dictators, cast
    kings, a disgraced president; some cashiered generals
And collapsed millionaires: we shall enact a play, I shall
    announce to the audience:
'All will be worse confounded soon.'

We shall beware of wild dogs in Europe, and of the police in
  armed imperial America:—
For all that pain was mainly a shift of power:—we shall
  enact our play: 'Oh Christian era,
Make a good end,' but first I announce to our audiences:
  'This play is prophetic, it will be centuries.
This play does not represent the world's end,
But only the fall of a civilization. It is not so late as you
  think: give nature time.'
In Europe we shall beware of starving dogs and political
  commissars, and of the police in America.
We shall rant on our makeshift stages in our cracked voices:
  'Oh Christian era,
Era of chivalry and the barbarians and the machines, era of
  science and the saints,
When you go down make a good sunset.
Never linger superfluous, old and holy and paralytic like
  India,
Go down in conclusive war and a great red sunset, great
  age go down,
For all will be worse confounded soon.'

We shall tour to the last verge and the open Pacific, we
  shall sit on the yellow cliffs at Hurricane Point
And watch the centaurs come from the sea; their splayed
  hooves plunge and stutter on the tide-rocks, watch
  them swarm up,
The hairy and foamy flanks, the naked destructive shoulders,
  the brutal faces and the bent bows,
Horde after horde under the screaming gulls: my old men
  will cough in the fog and baa like sheep,
'Here comes the end of a civilization. Give nature time,'
And spit, and make lewd jokes. But I shall laugh purely,
Remembering what old enthusiast named a girl's beauty and
  England's battle
Among the lights of his time: she being by then a dyed hag,
  or more likely

ROBIN-
SON
JEFFERS
One of those embalmer-fingered smiles in the subsoil; and
    England will be
Not admirable. I shall laugh purely, knowing the next age
Lives on not-human beauty, waiting on circumstance and its
    April, weaving its winter chrysalis;
Thin snow falls on historical rocks.

THE EYE

The Atlantic is a stormy moat, and the Mediterranean,
The blue pool in the old garden,
More than five thousand years has drunk sacrifice
Of ships and blood and shines in the sun; but here the
    Pacific:
The ships, planes, wars are perfectly irrelevant.
Neither our present blood-feud with the brave dwarfs
Nor any future world-quarrel of westering
And eastering man, the bloody migrations, greed of power,
    battle-falcons,
Are a mote of dust in the great scale-pan.
Here from this mountain shore, headland beyond stormy
    headland plunging like dolphins through the grey sea-
    smoke
Into pale sea, look west at the hill of water: it is half the
    planet: this dome, this half-globe, this bulging
Eyeball of water, arched over to Asia,
Australia and white Antarctica: those are the eyelids that
    never close; this is the staring unsleeping
Eye of the earth, and what it watches is not our wars.

Marianne Moore

(1888-   )

THE STEEPLE-JACK

Dürer would have seen a reason for living
     in a town like this, with eight stranded whales
to look at; with the sweet sea air coming into your house
on a fine day, from water etched
     with waves as formal as the scales
on a fish.

One by one, in two's, in three's, the seagulls keep
     flying back and forth over the town clock,
or sailing around the lighthouse without moving their
     wings—
rising steadily with a slight
     quiver of the body—or flock
mewing where

a sea the purple of the peacock's neck is
     paled to greenish azure as Dürer changed
the pine green of the Tyrol to peacock blue and guinea
grey. You can see a twenty-five-
     pound lobster and fish-nets arranged
to dry. The

whirlwind fife-and-drum of the storm bends the salt
     marsh grass, disturbs stars in the sky and the
star on the steeple; it is a privilege to see so
much confusion.

          A steeple-jack in red, has let
     a rope down as a spider spins a thread;

MARI-
ANNE
MOORE he might be part of a novel, but on the sidewalk a
sign says C. J. Poole, Steeple-Jack,
     in black and white; and one in red
and white says

Danger. The church portico has four fluted
     columns, each a single piece of stone, made
modester by white-wash. This would be a fit haven for
waifs, children, animals, prisoners,
     and presidents who have repaid
sin-driven

senators by not thinking about them. One
     sees a school-house, a post-office in a
store, fish-houses, hen-houses, a three-masted schooner on
the stocks. The hero, the student,
     the steeple-jack, each in his way,
is at home.

It scarcely could be dangerous to be living
     in a town like this, of simple people
who have a steeple-jack placing danger-signs by the church
when he is gilding the solid-
     pointed star, which on a steeple
stands for hope.

MELANCTHON

Openly, yes,
with the naturalness
    of the hippopotamus or the alligator
      when it climbs out on the bank to experience the

sun, I do these
things which I do, which please

no one but myself. Now I breathe and now I am sub-
merged; the blemishes stand up and shout when the
    object

in view was a
renaissance; shall I say
    the contrary? The sediment of the river which
    encrusts my joints, makes me very grey but I am used

to it, it may
remain there; do away
    with it and I am myself done away with, for the
    patina of circumstance can but enrich what was

there to begin
with. This elephant-skin
    which I inhabit, fibred over like the shell of
    the cocoanut, this piece of black glass through which no
        light

can filter—cut
into checkers by rut
    upon rut of unpreventable experience—
    it is a manual for the peanut-tongued and the

hairy-toed. Black
but beautiful, my back
    is full of the history of power. Of power? What
    is powerful and what is not? My soul shall never

be cut into
by a wooden spear; through-
    out childhood to the present time, the unity of
    life and death has been expressed by the circumference

described by my
trunk; nevertheless I
    perceive feats of strength to be inexplicable after
    all; and I am on my guard; external poise, it

has its centre
well nurtured—we know
   where—in pride; but spiritual pose, it has its centre
      where?
My ears are sensitized to more than the sound of

the wind. I see
and I hear, unlike the
   wandlike body of which one hears so much, which was
      made
   to see and not to see; to hear and not to hear;

that tree-trunk without
roots, accustomed to shout
   its own thoughts to itself like a shell, maintained intact
   by who knows what strange pressure of the atmosphere;
      that

spiritual
brother to the coral-
   plant, absorbed into which, the equable sapphire light
   becomes a nebulous green. The I of each is to

the I of each
a kind of fretful speech
   which sets a limit on itself; the elephant is
black earth preceded by a tendril? Compared with those

phenomena
which vacillate like a
   translucence of the atmosphere, the elephant is
   that on which darts cannot strike decisively the first

time, a substance
needful as an instance
   of the indestructibility of matter; it
   has looked at electricity and at the earth-

quake and is still
here; the name means thick. Will
    depth be depth, thick skin be thick, to one who can see
      no
beautiful element of unreason under it?

ENGLAND

with its baby rivers and little towns, each with its abbey or
    its cathedral,
with voices—one voice perhaps, echoing through the tran-
    sept—the
criterion of suitability and convenience; and Italy with its
    equal
shores—contriving an epicureanism from which the gross-
    ness has been

extracted: and Greece with its goat and its gourds, the nest
    of modified illusions:
and France, the 'chrysalis of the nocturnal butterfly', in
whose products mystery of construction diverts one from
    what was originally one's
object—substance at the core: and the East with its snails,
    its emotional

shorthand and jade cockroaches, its rock crystal and its im-
    perturbability,
all of museum quality: and America where there
is the little old ramshackle victoria in the south, where
    cigars are smoked on the
street in the north; where there are no proof-readers, no
    silk-worms, no digressions;

the wild man's land; grassless, linksless, languageless coun-
    try in which letters are written

not in Spanish, not in Greek, not in Latin, not in shorthand,
but in plain American which cats and dogs can read! The
letter *a* in psalm and calm when
pronounced with the sound of *a* in candle, is very noticeable,
but

why should continents of misapprehension have to be ac-
counted for by the
fact? Does it follow that because there are poisonous toad-
stools
which resemble mushrooms, both are dangerous? In the
case of mettlesomeness which may be
mistaken for appetite, of heat which may appear to be haste,
no con-

clusions may be drawn. To have misapprehended the matter
is to have confessed
that one has not looked far enough. The sublimated wisdom
of China, Egyptian discernment, the cataclysmic torrent of
emotion compressed
in the verbs of the Hebrew language, the books of the man
who is able

to say, 'I envy nobody but him, and him only, who catches
more fish than
I do',—the flower and fruit of all that noted superi-
ority—should one not have stumbled upon it in America,
must one imagine
that it is not there? It has never been confined to one locality.

A GRAVE

Man looking into the sea,
taking the view from those who have as much right to it as
    you have to it yourself,
it is human nature to stand in the middle of a thing,
but you cannot stand in the middle of this;
the sea has nothing to give but a well excavated grave.
The firs stand in a procession, each with an emerald turkey-
    foot at the top,
reserved as their contours, saying nothing;
repression, however, is not the most obvious characteristic
    of the sea;
the sea is a collector, quick to return a rapacious look.
There are others besides you who have worn that look—
whose expression is no longer a protest; the fish no longer
    investigate them
for their bones have not lasted:
men lower nets, unconscious of the fact that they are dese-
    crating a grave,
and row quickly away—the blades of the oars
moving together like the feet of water-spiders as if there
    were no such thing as death.
The wrinkles progress among themselves in a phalanx—
    beautiful under networks of foam,
and fade breathlessly while the sea rustles in and out of the
    seaweed;
the birds swim through the air at top speed, emitting cat-
    calls as heretofore—
the tortoise-shell scourges about the feet of the cliffs, in
    motion beneath them;
and the ocean, under the pulsation of lighthouses and noise
    of bell-buoys,
advances as usual, looking as if it were not that ocean in
    which dropped things are bound to sink—
in which if they turn and twist, it is neither with volition
    nor consciousness.

MARI-
ANNE
MOORE
Another armoured animal—scale
    lapping scale with spruce-cone regularity until they
form the uninterrupted central
    tail-row! This near artichoke with head and legs and
        grit-equipped gizzard,
the night miniature artist engineer is
    Leonardo's—da Vinci's replica—
        impressive animal and toiler of whom we seldom
        hear.
Armour seems extra. But for him,
    the closing ear-ridge—
        or bare ear lacking even this small
        eminence and similarly safe

contracting nose and eye apertures
    impenetrably closable, are not;—a true ant-eater,
not cockroach-eater, who endures
    exhausting solitary trips through unfamiliar ground at
        night,
returning before sunrise; stepping in the moonlight,
    on the moonlight peculiarly, that the outside
        edges of his hands may bear the weight and save
        the claws
for digging. Serpentined about
    the tree, he draws
        away from danger unpugnaciously,
        with no sound but a harmless hiss; keeping

the fragile grace of the Thomas-
    of-Leighton Buzzard Westminster Abbey wrought-
        iron vine, or
rolls himself into a ball that has
power to defy all effort to unroll it; strongly intailed,
        neat

head for core, on neck not breaking off, with curled-in
    feet.
     Nevertheless he has sting-proof scales; and nest
       of rocks closed with earth from inside, which he
       can thus darken
Sun and moon and day and night and man and beast
     each with a splendour
       which man in all his vileness cannot
       set aside; each with an excellence!

'Fearful yet to be feared,' the armoured
    ant-eater met by the driver-ant does not turn back, but
engulfs what he can, the flattened sword-
    edged leafpoints on the tail and artichoke set leg- and
       body-plates
quivering violently when it retaliates
     and swarms on him. Compact like the furled
       fringed frill
       on the hat-brim of Gargallo's hollow iron head
       of a
matador, he will drop and will
       then walk away
     unhurt, although if unintruded on,
     he cautiously works down the tree, helped

by his tail. The giant-pangolin-
    tail, graceful tool, as prop or hand or broom or axe,
       tipped like
the elephant's trunk with special skin,
    is not lost on this ant- and stone-swallowing uninjurable
    artichoke which simpletons thought a living fable
       whom the stones had nourished, whereas ants had
       done
       so. Pangolins are not aggressive animals; between
     dusk and day they have the not unchain-like machine-
       like

form and frictionless creep of a thing
made graceful by adversities, con-

versities. To explain grace requires
a curious hand. If that which is at all were not forever,
why would those who graced the spires
with animals and gathered there to rest, on cold luxurious
low stone seats—a monk and monk and monk—between
the thus
ingenious roof-supports, have slaved to confuse
grace with a kindly manner, time in which to pay
a debt,
the cure for sins, a graceful use
of what are yet
approved stone mullions branching out across
the perpendiculars ? A sailboat

was the first machine. Pangolins, made
for moving quietly also, are models of exactness,
on four legs ; or hind feet plantigrade,
with certain postures of a man. Beneath sun and moon,
man slaving
to make his life more sweet, leaves half the flowers
worth having,
needing to choose wisely how to use the strength ;
a paper-maker like the wasp ; a tractor of food-
stuffs,
like the ant ; spidering a length
of web from bluffs
above a stream ; in fighting, mechanicked
like the pangolin ; capsizing in

disheartenment. Bedizened or stark
naked, man, the self, the being we call human, writing-
master to this world, griffons a dark
'Like does not like like that is obnoxious' ; and writes
error with four

r's. Among animals, one has a sense of humour,
　　　Humour saves a few steps, it saves years. Un-
　　　　　ignorant,
　　　　　modest and unemotional, and all emotion,
　　　he has everlasting vigour,
　　　　　power to grow,
　　　　　　though there are few creatures who can make one
　　　　　breathe faster and make one erecter.

Not afraid of anything is he,
　　　and then goes cowering forth, tread paced to meet an
　　　　　obstacle
at every step. Consistent with the
　　formula—warm blood, no gills, two pairs of hands and
　　　　　a few hairs—that
is a mammal ; there he sits in his own habitat,
　　　serge-clad, strong-shod. The prey of fear, he, always
　　　curtailed, extinguished, thwarted by the dusk,
　　　　　work partly done,
　　says to the alternating blaze,
　　　'Again the sun!
　　　　anew each day ; and new and new and new,
　　　　that comes into and steadies my soul.'

THE MIND IS AN ENCHANTING THING

　　　is an enchanted thing
　　　　like the glaze on a
　　katydid-wing
　　　　　subdivided by sun
　　　　　till the nettings are legion.
　　Like Gieseking playing Scarlatti ;

　　　like the apteryx-awl
　　　　as a beak, or the

kiwi's rain-shawl
            of haired feathers, the mind
            feeling its way as though blind,
walks along with its eyes on the ground.

It has memory's ear
        that can hear without
having to hear.
            Like the gyroscope's fall,
            truly unequivocal
because trued by regnant certainty,

it is a power of
        strong enchantment. It
is like the dove-
            neck animated by
            sun; it is memory's eye;
it's conscientious inconsistency.

It tears off the veil; tears
        the temptation, the
mist the heart wears,
            from its eyes,—if the heart
            has a face; it takes apart
dejection. It's fire in the dove-neck's

iridescence; in the
        inconsistencies
of Scarlatti.
            Inconfusion submits
            its confusion to proof; it's
not a Herod's oath that cannot change.

John Crowe Ransom

(1888-   )

VISION BY SWEETWATER

Go and ask Robin to bring the girls over
To Sweetwater, said my Aunt; and that was why
It was like a dream of ladies sweeping by
The willows, clouds, deep meadowgrass, and the river.

Robin's sisters and my Aunt's lily daughter
Laughed and talked, and tinkled as wrens
If there were a little colony all hens
To go walking by the steep turn of Sweetwater.

Let them alone, dear Aunt, just for one minute
Till I go fishing in the dark of my mind:
Where have I seen before, against the wind,
These bright virgins, robed and bare of bonnet,

Flowing with music of their strange quick tongue
And adventuring with delicate paces by the stream,—
Myself a child, old suddenly at the scream
From one of the white throats which it hid among?

BELLS FOR JOHN WHITESIDE'S DAUGHTER

There was such speed in her little body,
And such lightness in her footfall,
It is no wonder her brown study
Astonishes us all.

Her wars were bruited in our high window.
We looked among orchard trees and beyond,
Where she took arms against her shadow,
Or harried unto the pond

The lazy geese, like a snow cloud
Dripping their snow on the green grass,
Tricking and stopping, sleepy and proud,
Who cried in goose, Alas.

For the tireless heart within the little
Lady with rod that made them rise
From their noon apple-dreams and scuttle
Goose-fashion under the skies!

But now go the bells, and we are ready,
In one house we are sternly stopped
To say we are vexed at her brown study,
Lying so primly propped.

ANTIQUE HARVESTERS

(Scene: Of the Mississippi the bank sinister, and of the Ohio the bank sinister.)

Tawny are the leaves turned but they still hold,
And it is harvest; what shall this land produce?
A meagre hill of kernels, a runnel of juice;
Declension looks from our land, it is old.
Therefore let us assemble, dry, grey, spare,
And mild as yellow air.

'I hear the croak of a raven's funeral wing.'
The young men would be joying in the song
Of passionate birds; their memories are not long.
What is it thus rehearsed in sable? 'Nothing.'

Trust not but the old endure, and shall be older
Than the scornful beholder.

JOHN
CROWE
RANSOM

We pluck the spindling ears and gather the corn.
One spot has special yield? 'On this spot stood
Heroes and drenched it with their only blood.'
And talk meets talk, as echoes from the horn
Of the hunter—echoes are the old men's arts,
Ample are the chambers of their hearts.

Here come the hunters, keepers of a rite;
The horn, the hounds, the lank mares coursing by
Straddled with archetypes of chivalry;
And the fox, lovely ritualist, in flight
Offering his unearthly ghost to quarry;
And the fields, themselves to harry.

Resume, harvesters. The treasure is full bronze
Which you will garner for the Lady, and the moon
Could tinge it no yellower than does this noon;
But grey will quench it shortly—the field, men, **stones**.
Pluck fast, dreamers; prove as you amble slowly
Not less than men, not wholly.

Bare the arm, dainty youths, bend the knees
Under bronze burdens. And by an autumn tone
As by a grey, as by a green, you will have known
Your famous Lady's image; for so have these;
And if one say that easily will your hands
More prosper in other lands,

Angry as wasp-music be your cry then:
'Forsake the Proud Lady, of the heart of fire,
The look of snow, to the praise of a dwindled choir,
Song of degenerate spectres that were men?
The sons of the fathers shall keep her, worthy of
What these have done in love.'

True, it is said of our Lady, she ageth.
But see, if you peep shrewdly, she hath not stooped;
Take no thought of her servitors that have drooped,
For we are nothing; and if one talk of death—
Why, the ribs of the earth subsist frail as a breath
If but God wearieth.

JUDITH OF BETHULIA

Beautiful as the flying legend of some leopard
She had not yet chosen her great captain or prince
Depository to her flesh, and our defence;
And a wandering beauty is a blade out of its scabbard
You know how dangerous, gentlemen of threescore?
May you know it yet ten more.

Nor by process of veiling she grew the less fabulous.
Grey or blue veils, we were desperate to study
The invincible emanations of her white body,
And the winds at her ordered raiment were ominous.
Might she walk in the market, sit in the council of soldiers?
Only of the extreme elders

But a rare chance was the girl's then, when the Invader
Trumpeted from the south, and rumbled from the north,
Beleaguered the city from four quarters of the earth,
Our soldiery too craven and sick to aid her—
Where were the arms could countervail this horde?
Her beauty was the sword.

She sat with the elders, and proved on their blear visage
How bright was the weapon unrusted in her keeping,
While he lay surfeiting on their harvest heaping,
Wasting the husbandry of their rarest vintage—

And dreaming of the broad-breasted dames for concubine?
These floated on his wine.

He was lapped with bay-leaves, and grass and fumiter weed,
And from under the wine-film encountered his mortal
vision,
For even within his tent she accomplished his derision;
She loosed one veil and another, standing unafraid;
And he perished. Nor brushed her with even so much as a
daisy?
She found his destruction easy.

The heathen are all perished. The victory was furnished,
We smote them hiding in our vineyards, barns, annexes,
And now their white bones clutter the holes of foxes,
And the chieftain's head, with grinning sockets, and
varnished—
Is it hung on the sky with a hideous epitaphy?
No, the woman keeps the trophy.

May God send unto our virtuous lady her prince.
It is stated she went reluctant to that orgy,
Yet a madness fevers our young men, and not the clergy
Nor the elders have turned them unto modesty since.
Inflamed by the thought of her naked beauty with desire?
Yes, and chilled with fear and despair.

PAINTED HEAD

By dark severance the apparition head
Smiles from the air a capital on no
Column or a Platonic perhaps head
On a canvas sky depending from nothing;

Stirs up an old illusion of grandeur
By tickling the instinct of heads to be

Absolute and to try decapitation
And to play truant from the body bush;

But too happy and beautiful for those sorts
Of head (homekeeping heads are happiest)
Discovers maybe thirty unwidowed years
Of not dishonouring the faithful stem;

Is nameless and has authored for the evil
Historian headhunters neither book
Nor state and is therefore distinct from tart
Heads with crowns and guilty gallery heads;

So that the extravagant device of art
Unhousing by abstraction this once head
Was capital irony by a loving hand
That knew the no treason of a head like this;

Makes repentance in an unlovely head
For having vinegarly traduced the flesh
Till, the hurt flesh recusing, the hard egg
Is shrunken to its own deathlike surface;

And an image thus. The body bears the head
(So hardly one they terribly are two)
Feeds and obeys and unto please what end?
Not to the glory of tyrant head but to

The increase of body. Beauty is of body.
The flesh contouring shallowly on a head
Is a rock-garden needing body's love
And best bodiness to colorify

The big blue birds sitting and sea-shell flats
And caves, and on the iron acropolis
To spread the hyacinthine hair and rear
The olive garden for the nightingales.

Conrad Aiken

(1889-)

ANNIHILATION

While the blue noon above us arches,
And the poplar sheds disconsolate leaves,
Tell me again why love bewitches,
And what love gives.

Is it the trembling finger that traces
The eyebrow's curve, the curve of the cheek?
The mouth that quivers, when the hand caresses,
But cannot speak?

No, not these, not in these is hidden
The secret, more than in other things:
Not only the touch of a hand can gladden
Till the blood sings.

It is the leaf that falls between us,
The bells that murmur, the shadows that move,
The autumnal sunlight that fades upon us:
These things are love.

It is the 'No, let us sit here longer',
The 'Wait till tomorrow', the 'Once I knew—'
These trifles, said as I touch your finger,
And the clock strikes two.

The world is intricate, and we are nothing.
It is the complex world of grass,
A twig on the path, a look of loathing,
Feelings that pass—

These are the secret! And I could hate you,
When, as I lean for another kiss,
I see in your eyes that I do not meet you,
And that love is this.

Rock meeting rock can know love better
Than eyes that stare or lips that touch.
All that we know in love is bitter.
And it is not much.

SYSTOLE AND DIASTOLE

Thus systole addressed diastole,—
The heart contracting, with its grief of burden,
To the lax heart, with grief of burden gone.

Thus star to dead leaf speaks; thus cliff to sea;
And thus the spider, on a summer's day,
To the bright thistledown, trapped in the web.

No language leaps this chasm like a lightning:
Here is no message of assuagement, blown
From Ecuador to Greenland; here is only

A trumpet blast, that calls dead men to arms;
The granite's pity for the cloud; the whisper
Of time to space.

THE STEPPING STONES

CONRAD
AIKEN

At the first stepping-stone, the past of water—
the thought with blunt nose swimming against the stream—
the tail and fins rigid, the water cold,
the scales cold, the past cold and perfect—

at the second stepping-stone, the present of water,
fluid memory surrounding the cold wish—
weeds borne downward on the changing stream
thoughts in a dream on the scarred stones—

at the third stepping-stone, the stillborn step—
suspended poise of the becoming soul—
I was there, I am here, I will be there and gone,
not yet gone, but waiting to be gone—

at the third stepping-stone, the sense of water,
the perfect stream, breakless unchanging all—:
let us wait here, in the timelessness of un-willing,
and watch the past and present perpend the future . . .

At the fourth stepping-stone, it is another,—
that other, not ourself, who stands and remembers
the departed one, who stayed at the third stone,
who is now present with us like a ghost—

ghost of water, ghost of stone, ghost of weed,
that other, alas, who is but is not, was
and is, is dead but will be, will be borne
downstream forever past the later comers—

those who reach the fifth stone, or the sixth,
who wait there poised, remembering, the dead men
whose deaths will take us on from stone to stone
further across the perfect stream of water—

but never across, never to reach the last,
the final remembrance, the all-knowing shore—
where death looks backward from the shading tree,
and perfect stillness stares at perfect stream.

THE SOUNDING

Blue sky, blue noon, and the secret line is flung:
once more, the Mariner his sounding takes;
from heaven's blue bridge once more the Lead is swung,
and downward through the ethereal Ocean breaks

the divine Plummet and the invisible cord
past sun-drowned Vega, and Orion's Belt.
Now the unfathomed is fathomed with a Word:
Earth and this City, by their heartbeat felt.

Like a small lightning through the clouds' pale glooms,
at intervals unguessed by the faint sun,
down to this stony reef, the city, comes
that cord, unloosed so soundlessly to run;

and on the bridge that arches the unknown
the Master Mariner, his sounding sure,
carves in the ice: A kingdom overthrown—
man kills his children. But the birds endure.

Edna St. Vincent Millay

(1892-1950)

NEVER MAY THE FRUIT BE PLUCKED

Never, never may the fruit be plucked from the bough
And gathered into barrels.
He that would eat of love must eat it where it hangs.
Though the branches bend like reeds,
Though the ripe fruit splash in the grass or wrinkle on the
tree,
He that would eat of love may bear away with him
Only what his belly can hold,
Nothing in the apron,
Nothing in the pockets.
Never, never may the fruit be gathered from the bough
And harvested in barrels.
The winter of love is a cellar of empty bins,
In an orchard soft with rot.

THE BUCK IN THE SNOW

White sky, over the hemlocks bowed with snow,
Saw you not at the beginning of evening the antlered buck
and his doe
Standing in the apple-orchard? I saw them. I saw them
suddenly go,
Tails up, with long leaps lovely and slow,
Over the stone-wall into the wood of hemlocks bowed with
snow.

Now lies he here, his wild blood scalding the snow.
How strange a thing is death, bringing to his knees,
bringing to his antlers

EDNA ST.
VINCENT
MILLAY The buck in the snow.
How strange a thing,—a mile away by now, it may be,
Under the heavy hemlocks that as the moments pass
Shift their loads a little, letting fall a feather of snow—
Life, looking out attentive from the eyes of the doe.

IN THE GRAVE NO FLOWER

Here dock and tare.
But there
No flower.

Here beggar-ticks, 'tis true;
Here the rank-smelling
Thorn-apple,—and who
Would plant this by his dwelling?
Here every manner of weed
To mock the faithful harrow:
Thistles, that feed
None but the finches; yarrow,
Blue vervain, yellow charlock; here
Bindweed, that chokes the struggling year;
Broad plantain and narrow.

But there no flower.

The rye is vexed and thinned,
The wheat comes limping home,
By vetch and whiteweed harried, and the sandy bloom
Of the sour-grass; here
Dandelions,—and the wind
Will blow them everywhere.

Save there.
There
No flower.

TO A YOUNG POET

EDNA ST.
VINCENT
MILLAY

Time cannot break the bird's wing from the bird.
Bird and wing together
Go down, one feather.

No thing that ever flew,
Not the lark, not you,
Can die as others do.

John Peale Bishop

(1892-1944)

THIS DIM AND PTOLEMAIC MAN

For forty years, for forty-one,
Sparing the profits of the sun,
This farmer piled his meagre hoard
To buy at last a rattly Ford.

Now crouched on a scared smile he feels
Motion spurt beneath his heels,
Rheumatically intent shifts gears,
Unloosing joints of rustic years.

Morning light obscures the stars,
He swerves avoiding other cars,
Wheels with the road, does not discern
He eastward goes at every turn,

Nor how his aged limbs are hurled
Through all the motions of the world,
How wild past farms, past ricks, past trees,
He perishes toward Hercules.

Robert P. Tristram Coffin

(1892-1955)

THE FOG

He knew how Roman legions looked, for he
Had seen the Maine coast fogs march in from sea
For many years now, in the August days.
They came in mighty columns up the bays,
Tawny and grey and silver in the sun;
They trampled out the seaports one by one,
The islands and the woods, with their high hosts,
And pushed the world back inland from the coasts.

This little house was lost, these hills and dells,
Cows in a pasture faded into bells,
The world around a man closed in and in
Till nowhere was ten paces from his chin.
A man drew up and halted with a start
To be so close to his own beating heart
And left so to himself and wholly blind
To everything but what was in his mind.

This was the peril and the comfort, too,
A man who lived in such a region knew;
On any Summer's day, within an hour,
He might be blind and naked to a power
So vast, it might have come from stars unmade,
Undreamt of, even, making him afraid,
So mightier than the night that he could guess
How life was but a name for loneliness.

Archibald MacLeish

(1892-   )

COOK COUNTY

The northeast wind was the wind off the lake
Blowing the oak-leaves pale side out like
Aspen: blowing the sound of the surf far
Inland over the fences: blowing for
Miles over smell of the earth the lake smell in.

The southwest wind was thunder in afternoon.
You saw the wind first in the trumpet vine
And the green went white with the sky and the weather-
  vane
Whirled on the barn and the doors slammed all together.
After the rain in the grass we used to gather
Wind-fallen cold white apples.

       The west
Wind was the August wind, the wind over waste
Valleys, over the waterless plains where still
Were skulls of the buffalo, where in the sand stale
Dung lay of wild cattle. The west wind blew
Day after day as the winds on the plains blow
Burning the grass, turning the leaves brown, filling
Noon with the bronze of cicadas, far out falling
Dark on the colourless water, the lake where not
Waves were nor movement.

       The north wind was at night
When no leaves and the husk on the oak stirs
Only nor birds then. The north wind was stars
Over the whole sky and snow in the ways
And snow on the sand where in summer the water was . . .

WORDS IN TIME

ARCHI-
BALD
MACLEISH

Bewildered with the broken tongue
Of wakened angels in our sleep—
Then, lost the music that was sung
And lost the light time cannot keep!

There is a moment when we lie
Bewildered, wakened out of sleep,
When light and sound and all reply:
That moment time must tame and keep.

That moment, like a flight of birds
Flung from the branches where they sleep,
The poet with a beat of words
Flings into time for time to keep.

Samuel Greenberg

(1893-1917)

CONDUCT

By a peninsula the painter sat and
Sketched the uneven valley groves.
The apostle gave alms to the
Meek. The volcano burst
In fusive sulphur and hurled
Rocks and ore into the air—
Heaven's sudden change at
The drawing tempestuous,
Darkening shade of dense clouded hues.
The wanderer soon chose
His spot of rest; they bore the
Chosen hero upon their shoulders,
Whom they strangely admired, as
The beach-tide summer of people desired.

PEACE

The blue, faded purple, horizon mount
Seemed to bellow the valleys in mists
Of enriching, ensuing, divine shadowings . . .
Where may this be? Perhaps unpopulated
Crags of stepping rocks, where thought
Slumbers, inhaled thought, unbearing
Real earth that refines e'er the insects' muse.
Royalty defies the haunt they chose,
Therein mingles wild, perspective charm,
As immortals' thorny, entangled growth

'Mongst the field of oaks, pressing steep
Twilight's veil, Milky Way's fence; the deep
Lionized eagle hisses o'er this scene;
Birds, wild swans, glide palely o'er a charming stream.

SAMUEL
GREEN-
BERG

MAN

Always alone, star-told?
What tales are bone and skulls?
O thou nigh art a lost mind!
Quite true, we dug gold out
Of thee. Wilt thou build shadows?
Cause them thicker than now?
A trip to the moon perhaps
Will turn Heaven's eye real.
O burning statue of tendons—
Time loses thine eye!

Dorothy Parker

(1893-   )

BOHEMIA

Authors and actors and artists and such
Never know nothing, and never know much.
Sculptors and singers and those of their kidney
Tell their affairs from Seattle to Sidney.
Playwrights and poets and such horses' necks
Start off from anywhere, end up at sex.
Diarists, critics, and similar roe
Never say nothing, and never say no.
People Who Do Things exceed my endurance ;
God, for a man that solicits insurance !

Mark Van Doren

(1894-   )

IT SHOULD BE EASY

It should be easy, letting the small feet go;
Quick should it turn, the necessary knob;
Empty this porch of any following eye
Fixed upon waves wherein a head shall bob
Now up, now down forever; till it rises,
And floats and disappears among the mob.

We should be sure the shoulders will return,
And the hands reach and click the lock again.
We should be thoughtless, occupying days
With a new ritual modified to men.
We should be proud and let a trumpet say
How close the waters welter about the den.

And solitude would soothe us, were it not
For the slow sound of breakers near the door:
Reminders of the many farther out,
Of the lost many, nameless evermore,
That young with pride set seaward long ago,
Leaving the grey alone, the mother shore.

It would be easy, letting the cap depart,
And the small face that never looks around;
But the firm coast line—suddenly it bends;
Suddenly it follows, and the sound
Of hopeless cries is heard; until the waves
Wash once again on straight and silent ground.

FORECLOSURE

So he sat down and slowly, slowly
Worked at his Christian name;
Watching the gold and halfway smiling
As the last letter came;
Till the whole sound was there, and shouted,
Suddenly, his shame.

Between this word then and the other—
His and his father's too—
He stared at the pen as if its handle
Were a great horn, and blew;
Then lowered the point and quietly laboured
Till the last ink was through.

So he got up, and through the wide silence
Wandered; and song began.
Not the old tune, for that was buried
Where the slow writing ran;
But remnants, hung in the wind awhile,
And impotent to scan.

There was the bell that once had brought him,
Frightened, across the field;
There was the mad white shepherd's barking,
And the hurt child, unhealed;
There was a hen whose blood came piping
To the red worm revealed.

There was quick trampling on a stairway,
Until doors sealed the sound.
There were the drums of winter booming
When the lame boy was drowned.
So his lost land went with him, pulling
Its tatters close around.

TALL TALE GOD

MARK
VAN
DOREN

If there were sound, the slapping
Of his reminded thigh,
The chuckle in the treetops—
As old, as high—
Would publish the true ages
Of our best brag and lie.

The colt that jumped North Mountain,
The macaroni dance;
The time we heard the breathing
Of boulders in a trance;
Midnight's lost meridians
Wheeling home from France;

The names we roared to rascals
Met on the back-hill road;
The insult at the picnic,
And how the children glowed;
The mica tree; the minted
Dollars in the lode—

He, long ago delighted,
Laughs now a double laugh:
At these, and at the wing-strength
Of so much dust and chaff;
The truth, he says, flew farther,
But not so high by half.

E. E. Cummings
(1894-   )

SEVEN POEMS

1

when life is quite through with
and leaves say alas,
much is to do
for the swallow, that closes
a flight in the blue;

when love's had his tears out,
perhaps shall pass
a million years
(while a bee dozes
on the poppies, the dears;

when all's done and said, and
under the grass
lies her head
by oaks and roses
deliberated.)

my father moved through dooms of love
through sames of am through haves of give,
singing each morning out of each night
my father moved through depths of height

this motionless forgetful where
turned at his glance to shining here;
that if (so timid air is firm)
under his eyes would stir and squirm

newly as from unburied which
floats the first who, his april touch
drove sleeping selves to swarm their fates
woke dreamers to their ghostly roots

and should some why completely weep
my father's fingers brought her sleep:
vainly no smallest voice might cry
for he could feel the mountains grow.

Lifting the valleys of the sea
my father moved through griefs of joy;
praising a forehead called the moon
singing desire into begin

joy was his song and joy so pure
a heart of star by him could steer
and pure so now and now so yes
the wrists of twilight would rejoice

keen as midsummer's keen beyond
conceiving mind of sun will stand,
so strictly (over utmost him
so hugely) stood my father's dream

his flesh was flesh his blood was blood:
no hungry man but wished him food;
no cripple wouldn't creep one mile
uphill to only see him smile.

Scorning the pomp of must and shall
my father moved through dooms of feel;
his anger was as right as rain
his pity was as green as grain

septembering arms of year extend
less humbly wealth to foe and friend
than he to foolish and to wise
offered immeasurable is

proudly and (by octobering flame
beckoned) as earth will downward climb,
so naked for immortal work
his shoulders marched against the dark

his sorrow was as true as bread:
no liar looked him in the head;
if every friend became his foe
he'd laugh and build a world with snow.

My father moved through theys of we,
singing each new leaf out of each tree
(and every child was sure that spring
danced when she heard my father sing)

then let men kill which cannot share,
let blood and flesh be mud and mire,
scheming imagine, passion willed,
freedom a drug that's bought and sold

giving to steal and cruel kind,
a heart to fear, to doubt a mind,

to differ a disease of same,
conform the pinnacle of am

though dull were all we taste as bright,
bitter all utterly things sweet,
maggoty minus and dumb death
all we inherit, all bequeath

and nothing quite so least as truth
—i say though hate were why men breathe—
because my father lived his soul
love is the whole and more than all

3

might these be thrushes climbing through almost (do they

beautifully wandering in merciful
miracles wonderingly celebrate day
and welcome earth's arrival with a soul)

sunlight? yes
                (always we have heard them sing
the dark alive but)
                        look: begins to grow
more than all real, all imagining;

and we who are we? surely not i not you
behold nor any breathing creature this?
nothing except the impossible shall occur

—see! now himself uplifts of stars the star
(sing! every joy)—wholly now disappear
night's not eternal terrors like a guess.

Life's life and strikes my your our blossoming sphere

Pity this busy monster, manunkind,

not. Progress is a comfortable disease:
your victim (death and life safely beyond)

plays with the bigness of his littleness
—electrons deify one razorblade
into a mountainrange; lenses extend

unwish through curving wherewhen till unwish
returns on its unself.
           A world of made
is not a world of born—pity poor flesh

and trees, poor stars and stones, but never this
fine specimen of hypermagical

ultraomnipotence. We doctors know

a hopeless case if—listen: there's a hell
of a good universe next door; let's go

5

It was a goodly co
which paid to make man free
(for man is enslaved by a dread dizziz
and the sooner it's over the sooner to biz
don't ask me what it's pliz

then up rose bishop budge from kew
a anglican was who
(with a rag and a bone and a hank of hair)'d
he picked up a thousand pounds or two
and he smote the monster merde

then up rose pride and up rose pelf
and ghibelline and guelph
and ladios and laddios
(on radios and raddios)
did save man from himself

ye duskiest despot's goldenest gal
did wring that dragon's tail
(for men must loaf and women must lay)
and she gave him a desdemonial
that took his breath away

all history oped her teeming womb
said demon for to doom
yea (fresh complexions being oke
with him) one william shakespeare broke
the silence of the tomb

then up rose mr lipshits pres
(who always nothing says)
and he kisséd the general menedjerr
and they smokéd a robert burns cigerr
to the god of things like they err

6

plato told

him: he couldn't
believe it (jesus

told him; he
wouldn't believe
it) lao

tsze
certainly told

him, and general
(yes

mam)
sherman;
and even
(believe it
or

not) you
told him: i told
him; we told him
(he didn't believe it, no

sir) it took
a nipponized bit of
the old sixth

avenue
el; in the top of his head: to tell

him

7

noone" autumnal this great lady's gaze

enters a sunset "can grow (gracefully or
otherwise) old. Old may mean anything
which everyone would rather not become;
but growing is" erect her whole life smiled

"was and will always remain: who i am.

Look at these (each serenely welcoming
his only and illimitably his
destiny) mountains! how can each" while flame
crashed "be so am and i and who? each grows"

then in a whisper, as time turned to dream

"and poets grow; and (there—see?) children" nor
might any earth's first morning have concealed
so unimaginably young a star

Rolfe Humphries

(1895-   )

RENDER UNTO CÆSAR

One side of the coin has a vicious monarch's face,—
His image and superscription written plain—
Evil and tyrannous. The other side
Has a crown of laurel, and stars, and a field of sky.

Nobody, taking the coin from purse or pocket,
Holding its weight in the hollow of the hand,
Ever wonders which side is the more important,
Which is the one that makes it legal tender.
The only question is this one, very simple:
What will the money buy?

Hard and durable metal. Centuries after
Its empire crumbles, the disk and the imprint keep
Their mark, their shape, under the ash and rubble,
Under the loam, unearthed some day, and studied,
Rubbed bright again, the tyrant and the laurel,
Placed under glass in an up-to-date museum,
Current no longer, coin of the realm no more,
Purchasing power lost, but the value greater,
Greater than any it ever had before.

THE CYNNEDDF

After a banquet
Powyll of Dyfed
With many attending

Strolled to hillock
Back of the palace.

'Lord,' said a courtier,
'Here is a strangeness:
If you sit on this mound
One of two things
Will certainly happen
Before you depart,
The hurt of a wound,
Or the sight of a wonder.'

'I fear no wound,'
Said Powyll of Dyfed,
'With this host all around me,
And as for a wonder,
Gladly I'd see one,
For wonders were ever
Dear to my heart.'

He sat on the mound,
And a lady came riding,
Lovely to look at
In garments of gold
On a cream-coloured stallion.
She rode very slowly,
She sang sweet and low,
And no one there knew her.

Powyll of Dyfed
Followed on foot
And could not overtake her,
And sent for the sorrel,
Most fleet of his stable,
Mounted and rode
By cairn and by cromlech.

Salmon and eagle,
The owl and the ousel,
From rock and from river,
From water, from air,
Watched the pursuit,
Pursued and pursuer.

Weary of riding,
Powyll of Dyfed
Cried in despair
To the beautiful lady,
'Stay, in the name
Of the one you love best!'
She reined in, smiling,
Turned to him, told him,
'Had you said so the sooner,
You would have spared
Your spirited sorrel
A great deal of anguish,'
And she took off her veil.

Of all of the maidens
And all of the women
He ever had seen
This was the fairest.
Powyll of Dyfed
Came to her side,
Said to her, 'Lady,
Receive my greeting,
And what is your journey?'
—'I go my own errand
In my own manner,'
—'Oh, what is your quest?'
—'You,' she replied.

It would be a big lie
To say they were happy

For ever and ever:
Boredom, depression,
Sometimes would settle
Even in Narberth,
And now and again
The hurt of a wound
That time could not always
Stifle or soften:
But every so often,
And over and over,
They would see from the mound
A wonder go by.

ROLFE
HUMPH-
RIES

Edmund Wilson

(1895-   )

ON EDITING SCOTT FITZGERALD'S PAPERS

Scott, your last fragments I arrange tonight,
Assigning commas, setting accents right,
As once I punctuated, spelled and trimmed
When, passing in a Princeton spring—how dimmed
By this damned quarter-century and more!—
You left your *Shadow Laurels* at my door.
That was a drama webbed of dreams: the scene
A shimmering beglamoured bluish-green
Soiled Paris wineshop; the sad hero one
Who loved applause but had his life alone;
Who fed on drink for weeks; forgot to eat,
'Worked feverishly,' nourished on defeat
A lyric pride, and lent a lyric voice
To all the tongueless knavish tavern-boys,
The liquor-ridden, the illiterate;
Got stabbed one midnight by a tavern mate—
Betrayed, but self-betrayed by stealthy sins—
And faded to the sound of violins.

Tonight, in this dark long Atlantic gale,
I set in order such another tale,
While tons of wind that take the world for scope
Rock blackened waters where marauders grope
Our blue and bathed-in Massachusetts ocean;
The Cape shakes with the depth-bomb's dumbed con-
    cussion;
And guns can interrupt me in these rooms,
Where now I seek to breathe again the fumes

Of iridescent drinking-dens, retrace
The bright hotels, regain the eager pace
You tell of . . . Scott, the bright hotels turn bleak;
The pace limps or stamps; the wines are weak;
The horns and violins come faint tonight.
A rim of darkness that devours light
Runs like the wall of flame that eats the land;
Blood, brain and labour pour into the sand;

I climbed, a quarter-century and more
Played out, my college steps, unlatched my door,
And, creature strange to college, found you there:
The pale skin, hard green eyes, and yellow hair—
Intently pinching out before a glass
Some pimples left by parties at the Nass;
Nor did you stop abashed, thus pocked and blotched,
But kept on peering while I stood and watched.
Tonight, from days more distant now, we find,
Than holidays in France were, left behind,
Than spring of graduation from the fall
That saw us grubbing below City Hall,
Through storm and darkness, Time's contrary stream,
There glides amazingly your mirror's beam—
To bring before me still, glazed mirror-wise,
The glitter of the hard and emerald eyes.
The cornea tough, the aqueous chamber cold,
Those glassy optic bulbs that globe and hold—
They pass their image on to what they mint,
To blue ice or light buds attune their tint
And leave us, to turn over, iris-fired,
Not the great Ritz-sized diamond you desired
But jewels in a handful, lying loose:
Flawed amethysts; the moonstone's milky blues;
Chill blues of pale transparent tourmaline;
Opals of shifty yellow, chartreuse green,
Wherein a vein vermilion flees and flickers—
Tight phials of the spirit's light mixed liquors;

Some tinsel zircons, common turquoise; but
Two emeralds, green and lucid, one half-cut,
One cut consummately—both take their place
In Letters' most expensive Cartier case.

And here, among our comrades of the trade,
Some buzz like husks, some stammer, much afraid,
Some mellowly give tongue and join the drag
Like hounds that bay the bounding anise-bag,
Some swallow darkness and sit hunched and dull,
The stunned beast's stupor in the monkey-skull.
And there I have set them out for final show,
And come to the task's dead-end, and dread to know
Those eyes struck dark, dissolving in a wrecked
And darkened world, that gleam of intellect
That spilled into the spectrum of tune, taste,
Scent, colour, living speech, is gone, is lost;
And we must dwell among the ragged stumps,
With owls digesting mice to dismal lumps
Of skin and gristle, monkeys scared by thunder,
Great buzzards that descend to grab the plunder.
And I, your scraps and sketches sifting yet,
Can never thus revive one sapphire jet
However close I look, however late,
But only spell and point and punctuate.

Louise Bogan

(1897-   )

BAROQUE COMMENT

From loud sound and still chance;
From mindless earth, wet with a dead million leaves;
From the forest, the empty desert, the tearing beasts,
The kelp-disordered beaches;
Coincident with the lie, anger, lust, oppression and death in
    many forms:

Ornamental structures, continents apart, separated by seas;
Fitted marble, swung bells; fruit in garlands as well as on the
    branch;
The flower at last in bronze, stretched backward, or curled
    within;
Stone in various shapes: beyond the pyramid, the contrived
    arch and the buttress;
The named constellations;
Crown and vesture; palm and laurel chosen as noble and
    enduring;
Speech proud in sound; death considered sacrifice;
Mask, weapon, urn; the ordered strings;
Fountains, foreheads under weather-bleached hair;
The wreath, the oar, the tool,
The prow;
The turned eyes and the opened mouth of love.

LOUISE
BOGAN

M., SINGING

Now, innocent, within the deep
Night of all things you turn the key
Unloosing what we know in sleep.
In your fresh voice they cry aloud
Those beings without heart or name.

Those creatures both corrupt and proud,
Upon the melancholy words
And in the music's subtlety,
Leave the long harvest which they reap
In the sunk land of dust and flame
And move to space beneath our sky.

John Wheelright

(1897-1940)

WHY MUST YOU KNOW?

—'What was that sound we heard
fall on the snow?'
—'It was a frozen bird.
Why must you know?
All the dull earth knows the good
that the air, with claws and wings
tears to the scattered questionings
which burn in fires of our blood.'
—'Let the air's beak and claws
    carry my deeds
far, where no springtime thaws,
    the frost for their seeds.'
—'One could fathom every sound
that the circling blood can tell
who heard the diurnal syllable,
while lying close against the ground.'
—'My flesh, bone and sinew
    now would discern
hidden waters in you
    Earth, waters that burn.'
—'One who turns to earth again
finds solace in its weight; and deep
hears the blood forever keep
the silence between drops of rain.'

THE HUNTSMAN

My cartridge belt is empty.
I have killed no beasts.
I have one bullet.
Can we; with untrembled pistol
when a serpent clasps a child;
send the bullet through the serpent
past the small head of the child?
Be not disconsolate if the bullet
pierce both child and serpent.
A trembled pistol spares the serpent
to kill the child.
Throw the empty belt away.
Take the pistol.
Shoot

PAUL AND VIRGINIA

Nephews and Nieces,—love your leaden statues.
Call them by name; call him 'Paul'. She is 'Virginia'.
He leans on his spade. Virginia fondles a leaden
fledgling in its nest. Paul fondles with his Eyes.
You need no cast in words. You know the Statues,
but not their Lawns; nor words to plant again
the shade trees, felled; ponds, filled, and built over.
Your Garden is destroyed, but there are other Gardens
yet to spare from the destroying Spoor
unseen, save in destructful Acts. Unseen
a hungered Octopus crawls under ground
as Fungus; eats the air as Orchids on all trees;
and on all waters spreads translucent Slime.
Nephews and Nieces, who would breathe sweet Air
and till rich Ground, spy out against its suction;
wither these spreading tentacles, these roots
and radicles of cancerous Greed.

Let us put Paul and Virginia back in the Garden's
warmth of wet Box and Arbor Vitae. The Bell-Tree
a silver shrub from Japan, is grown up Big
like a willow whose Branches nose the Ground. They root
and eat the Earth. They drink deep water springs
while finger twigs fill neighbouring winds with silent
tinkles of Petals, blowing on Lilies-of-the-Valley
on Larches, on copper Beeches, urn-like Elms
on Lilies, Iris, Roses walled with Hedges
mirrored on dark waters and, light with fruit trees,
on Peonies abiding in quiet pomp with leaden
Statues in a Garden, alive with Bugs and Toads.
This Garden, sad as a ripe joy is sad (dead Garden)
sheds no perfume of Soil, over a soil-less land.
This dead Garden's seeds take root in children
like the Cherry a young girl swallowed,—Stem,
Meat, and Stone; to bud, to bloom, to fruit
and to house twittering Birds.

In your Mother and Father, much you love is memory;
and much they love in you is memory transplanted
from Gardens of Love, which speak to Love from a dead
world to another, and from Death, which speaks to life
through love remembered. Nephews and Nieces,—love
your Statues, love their names.

Stephen Vincent Benet

(1897-1943)

INVOCATION

American muse, whose strong and diverse heart
So many men have tried to understand
But only made it smaller with their art,
Because you are as various as your land,

As mountainous-deep, as flowered with blue rivers,
Thirsty with deserts, buried under snows,
As native as the shape of Navajo quivers,
And native, too, as the sea-voyaged rose.

Swift runner, never captured or subdued,
Seven-branched elk beside the mountain stream,
That half a hundred hunters have pursued
But never matched their bullets with the dream,

Where the great huntsmen failed, I set my sorry
And mortal snare for your immortal quarry.

You are the buffalo-ghost, the broncho-ghost
With dollar-silver in your saddle-horn,
The cowboys riding in from Painted Post,
The Indian arrow in the Indian corn,

And you are the clipped velvet of the lawns
Where Shropshire grows from Massachusetts sods,
The grey Maine rocks—and the war-painted dawns
That break above the Garden of the Gods.

The prairie-schooners crawling toward the ore
And the cheap car, parked by the station-door.

Where the skyscrapers lift their foggy plumes
Of stranded smoke out of a stony mouth
You are that high stone and its arrogant fumes,
And you are the ruined gardens in the South

And bleak New England farms, so winter-white
Even their roofs look lonely, and the deep
The middle grainland where the wind of night
Is like all blind earth sighing in her sleep

A friend, an enemy, a sacred hag
With two tied oceans in her medicine-bag.

They tried to fit you with an English song
And clip your speech into the English tale.
But, even from the first, the words went wrong,
The catbird pecked away the nightingale.

The homesick men begot high-cheekboned things
Whose wit was whittled with a different sound
And Thames and all the rivers of the kings
Ran into Mississippi and were drowned.

They planted England with a stubborn trust.
But the cleft dust was never English dust.

Stepchild of every exile from content
And all the disavouched, hard-bitten pack
Shipped overseas to steal a continent
With neither shirts nor honour to their back.

Pimping grandee and rump-faced regicide,
Apple-cheeked younkers from a windmill-square,

STEPHEN
VINCENT
BENET
Puritans stubborn as the nails of Pride,
Rakes from Versailles and thieves from County Clare,

The black-robed priests who broke their hearts in vain
To make you God and France or God and Spain.

These were your lovers in your buckskin-youth.
And each one married with a dream so proud
He never knew it could not be the truth
And that he coupled with a girl of cloud.

And now to see you is more difficult yet
Except as an immensity of wheel
Made up of wheels, oiled with inhuman sweat
And glittering with the heat of ladled steel.

All these you are, and each is partly you,
And none is false, and none is wholly true.

So how to see you as you really are,
So how to suck the pure, distillate, stored
Essence of essence from the hidden star
And make it pierce like a riposting sword

For, as we hunt you down, you must escape
And we pursue a shadow of our own
That can be caught in a magician's cape
But has the flatness of a painted stone.

Never the running stag, the gull at wing,
The pure elixir, the American thing.

And yet, at moments when the mind was hot
With something fierier than joy or grief,
When each known spot was an eternal spot
And every leaf was an immortal leaf,

I think that I have seen you, not as one,
But clad in diverse semblances and powers
Always the same, as light falls from the sun,
And always different, as the differing hours.

STEPHEN
VINCENT
BENET

Yet, through each altered garment that you wore
The naked body, shaking the heart's core.

All day the snow fell on that Eastern town
With its soft, pelting, little, endless sigh
Of infinite flakes that brought the tall sky down
Till I could put my hands in the white sky

And taste cold scraps of heaven on my tongue
And walk in such a changed and luminous light
As gods inhabit when the gods are young.
All day it fell. And when the gathered night

Was a blue shadow cast by a pale glow
I saw you then, snow-image, bird of the snow.

And I have seen and heard you in the dry
Close-huddled furnace of the city street
When the parched moon was planted in the sky
And the limp air hung dead against the heat

I saw you rise, red as that rusty plant,
Dizzied with lights, half-mad with senseless sound,
Enormous metal, shaking to the chant
Of a triphammer striking iron ground.

Enormous power, ugly to the fool,
And beautiful as a well-handled tool.

These, and the memory of that windy day
On the bare hills, beyond the last barbed wire,

STEPHEN
VINCENT
BENET

When all the orange poppies bloomed one way
As if a breath would blow them into fire,

I keep forever, like the sea-lion's tusk
The broken sailor brings away to land,
But when he touches it, he smells the musk,
And the whole sea lies hollow in his hand.

So, from a hundred visions, I make one,
And out of darkness build my mocking sun.

And should that task seem fruitless in the eyes
Of those a different magic sets apart
To see through the ice-crystal of the wise
No nation but the nation that is Art,

Their words are just. But when the birchbark-call
Is shaken with the sound that hunters make
The moose comes plunging through the forest-wall
Although the rifle waits beside the lake.

Art has no nations—but the mortal sky
Lingers like gold in immortality.

This flesh was seeded from no foreign grain
But Pennsylvania and Kentucky wheat,
And it has soaked in California rain
And five years tempered in New England sleet

To strive at last, against an alien proof
And by the changes of an alien moon,
To build again that blue, American roof
Over a half-forgotten battle-tune

And call unsurely, from a haunted ground,
Armies of shadows and the shadow-sound.

In your Long House there is an attic-place STEPHEN
VINCENT
BENET
Full of dead epics and machines that rust,
And there, occasionally, with casual face,
You come awhile to stir the sleepy dust;

Neither in pride nor mercy, but in vast
Indifference at so many gifts unsought,
The yellowed satins, smelling of the past,
And all the loot the lucky pirates brought.

I only bring a cup of silver air,
Yet, in your casualness, receive it there.

Receive the dream too haughty for the breast,
Receive the words that should have walked as bold
As the storm walks along the mountain-crest
And are like beggars whining in the cold.

The maimed presumption, the unskilful skill,
The patchwork colours, fading from the first,
And all the fire that fretted at the will
With such a barren ecstasy of thirst.

Receive them all—and should you choose to touch them
With one slant ray of quick, American light,
Even the dust will have no power to smutch them,
Even the worst will glitter in the night.

If not—the dry bones littered by the way
May still point giants toward their golden prey.

Horace Gregory

(1899-   )

THE UNWILLING GUEST:
AN URBAN DIALOGUE

—How still, how very still the air is,
As though it waited, is still waiting
For the clock to strike. Did you see that shadow
Fall behind the clock, behind the white face
of the dial?

      —No.

—Will you have a drink?

              —No.

—Another cigarette?

           —No

—If I lift the curtain you can see
Three Spaniards, a Welsh Albino and a Levantine Greek
Drinking their hearts away. One wears
A newly rented evening gown. I can almost
Hear them singing. Did you say something?

                  —No.

—That's half the charm of living
In the city. Do you expect to stay here long?

                  —No.

—You must remember it is a holiday: the
Coronation of another half-century,
And nearly midnight. The snow is falling lightly,
Carefully drifting, yet the room is very warm:
'You could fancy we were lying
On the beach.' Do you want to sing?

                                —No.

—Do you find the room unnaturally quiet?

                                —No. It
Is probably trying to think. If anything waits
For something it cannot think.

—You mean it falls apart? But the room is still
Here. You can sit on the table or pace the floor
Or talk.

                —That is what I meant.
                                —Listen,
Is that a starling behind the chimney piece? Or water
     flowing?
I forgot to water the statues in the hall,
The three girls picking flowers, the little ones,
Called Morning, Noon, and Night. And the large ones,
Father and Mother, who sometimes talk,
Should be fed at once, then covered with a cloth
And put to sleep. One becomes extremely
Domestic if one lives alone.

                        —That fluttering
Of wings behind the walls could be echoes
Of a blind man playing a violin,
Or is everyone in the city blessed with eyes?
You needn't answer.

—There is a half-domed
Casement pouring light above us; it is not,
But looks like a three-quarter moon.
Would you like to see it?

—No.

—If I open the shades
You will see layers and layers of freshly cut
Plate glass, light splintering
The streets from a million windows.
And O the people! Everyone talking, laughing, dining out,
But you cannot hear them. Here is one window
Filled with dancing couples, and in another
Four children are playing cards, and in that window
I think I see the horseshow at a concert:
The usual pearls and gloves, white shirt front,
Naked shoulder, and minutely printed on a folded play-bill
Held in a woman's hand, *Roméo et Juliette*.
                                        And in the windows
Everything to sell: the latest inventions
In copper wire, spun brass, gun-cotton, steel,
Even uranium, each almost perfect of its kind,
Sharp, clean, reflecting light—O a million lights,
Flood lights out of the dark,
Cross-beamed, white, yellow, red against the sky.
Shall I open our window?

—No.

—Everything looks
As it has seemed for almost fifty years,
A trifle overbright, but ingenuous, cheerful,
Mindful of holidays: The Alexandrian city.
Do you remember Alexandria?

—No.

—Pharos?

      —No.

             —If I draw the shades
It is as peaceful as Pharos before the tower fell.
But we, of course, are on a different island,
Hearing other rumours, if we choose to hear them,
In the African silence of this room.
Shall I unroll a map? There are rumours
That all cities are fires dropped from the sky
In a curious geography of wars:
This shaded portion of the map was Pharos:
The gods no longer walk there.
                     And across the water
The grape withers and runs over
A mound of thistled grass, and look, the Pillar
Of Cestius is a pyramid of smoke.
                     There is nothing here
That the wind cannot blow away, except the harbours,
Except in the deeper forests perhaps
A cave. If you look too closely the map is
Like a lecture at a museum
That no one cares to hear. Is that shadow still
Wandering behind the clock? Even as you leave the room,
It is still a temporal hour:
It is excellent weather for a holiday.

Hart Crane

(1899-1932)

TO BROOKLYN BRIDGE

How many dawns, chill from his rippling rest
The seagull's wings shall dip and pivot him,
Shedding white rings of tumult, building high
Over the chained bay waters Liberty—

Then, with inviolate curve, forsake our eyes
As apparitional as sails that cross
Some page of figures to be filed away;
—Till elevators drop us from our day . . .

I think of cinemas, panoramic sleights
With multitudes bent toward some flashing scene
Never disclosed, but hastened to again,
Foretold to other eyes on the same screen;

And Thee, across the harbour, silver-paced
As though the sun took step of thee, yet left
Some motion ever unspent in thy stride,—
Implicitly thy freedom staying thee!

Out of some subway scuttle, cell or loft
A bedlamite speeds to thy parapets,
Tilting there momently, shrill shirt ballooning,
A jest falls from the speechless caravan.

Down Wall, from girder into street noon leaks,
A rip-tooth of the sky's acetylene;
All afternoon the cloud-flown derricks turn . . .
Thy cables breathe the North Atlantic still.

And obscure as that heaven of the Jews,
Thy guerdon . . . Accolade thou dost bestow
Of anonymity time cannot raise:
Vibrant reprieve and pardon thou dost show.

O harp and altar, of the fury fused,
(How could mere toil align thy choiring strings!)
Terrific threshold of the prophet's pledge,
Prayer of pariah, and the lover's cry,—

Again the traffic lights that skim thy swift
Unfractioned idiom, immaculate sigh of stars,
Beading thy path—condense eternity:
And we have seen night lifted in thine arms.

Under thy shadow by the piers I waited;
Only in darkness is thy shadow clear.
The City's fiery parcels all undone,
Already snow submerges an iron year . . .

O Sleepless as the river under thee,
Vaulting the sea, the prairies' dreaming sod,
Unto us lowliest sometime sweep, descend
And of the curveship lend a myth to God.

VAN WINKLE

Macadam, gun-grey as the tunny's belt,
Leaps from Far Rockaway to Golden Gate:
Listen! the miles a hurdy-gurdy grinds—
Down gold arpeggios mile on mile unwinds.

Times earlier, when you hurried off to school
—It is the same hour though a later day—
You walked with Pizarro in a copybook,

*Streets
spread past
store and
factory—
sped by sun-
light and her
smile . . .*

*Like
Memory, she
is time's
truant, shall
take you by
the hand . . .*

And Cortez rode up, reining tautly in—
Firmly as coffee grips the taste,—and away!

There was Priscilla's cheek close in the wind,
And Captain Smith, all beard and certainty,
And Rip Van Winkle bowing by the way,—
'Is this Sleepy Hollow, friend—?' And he—

*And Rip forgot the office hours, and he forgot the pay;
Van Winkle sweeps a tenement way down on Avenue A,—*

The grind-organ says . . . Remember, remember
The cinder pile at the end of the backyard
Where we stoned the family of young
Garter snakes under . . . And the monoplanes
We launched—with paper wings and twisted
Rubber bands . . . Recall-recall
                                    the rapid tongues
That flittered from under the ash heap day
After day whenever your stick discovered
Some sunning inch of unsuspecting fibre—
It flashed back at your thrust, as clean as fire.

*And Rip was slowly made aware
          that he, Van Winkle, was not here
     nor there. He woke and swore he'd seen Broadway
          a Catskill daisy chain in May—*

So memory, that strikes a rhyme out of a box
Or splits a random smell of flowers through glass—
Is it the whip stripped from the lilac tree
One day in spring my father took to me,
Or is it the Sabbatical, unconscious smile
My mother almost brought me once from church
And once only, as I recall—?

It flickered through the snow screen, blindly
It forsook her at the doorway, it was gone
Before I had left the window. It
Did not return with the kiss in the hall.

Macadam, gun-grey as the tunny's belt,
Leaps from Far Rockaway to Golden Gate. . . .
Keep hold of that nickel for car-change, Rip,—
Have you got your '*Times*'—?
And hurry along, Van Winkle—it's getting late!

(from THE BRIDGE)

THE SEA

Above the fresh ruffles of the surf
Bright striped urchins flay each other with sand.
They have contrived a conquest for shell shucks,
And their fingers crumble fragments of baked weed
Gaily digging and scattering.

And in answer to their treble interjections
The sun beats lightning on the waves,
The waves fold thunder on the sand;
And could they hear me I would tell them:

O brilliant kids, frisk with your dog,
Fondle your shells and sticks, bleached
By time and the elements; but there is a line
You must not cross nor ever trust beyond it
Spry cordage of your bodies to caresses
Too lichen-faithful from too wide a breast.
The bottom of the sea is cruel.

CHAPLINESQUE

We make our meek adjustments,
Contented with such random consolations
As the wind deposits
In slithered and too ample pockets.

For we can still love the world, who find
A famished kitten on the step, and know
Recesses for it from the fury of the street,
Or warm torn elbow coverts.

We will sidestep, and to the final smirk
Dally the doom of that inevitable thumb
That slowly chafes its puckered index toward us,
Facing the dull squint with what innocence
And what surprise!

And yet these fine collapses are not lies
More than the pirouettes of any pliant cane;
Our obsequies are, in a way, no enterprise.
We can evade you, and all else but the heart:
What blame to us if the heart live on.

The game enforces smirks; but we have seen
The moon in lonely alleys make
A grail of laughter of an empty ash can,
And through all sound of gaiety and quest
Have heard a kitten in the wilderness.

ISLAND QUARRY

HART
CRANE

Square sheets—they saw the marble into
Flat slabs there at the marble quarry
At the turning of the road around the roots of the mountain
Where the straight road would seem to ply below the stone,
    that fierce
Profile of marble spiked with yonder
Palms against the sunset's towering sea, and maybe
Against mankind. It is at times—

In dusk it as at times as though this island lifted, floated
In Indian baths. At Cuban dusk the eyes
Walking the straight road toward thunder—
This dry road silvering toward the shadow of the quarry
—It is at times as though the eyes burned hard and glad
And did not take the goat path quivering to the right,
Wide of the mountain—thence to tears and sleep—
But went on into marble that does not weep.

Allen Tate

(1899-   )

SEASONS OF THE SOUL

To the memory of John Peale Bishop, 1892-1944

Allor porsi la mano un poco avante
e colsi un ramicel da un gran pruno ;
e il tronco suo grido : Perchè mi schiante?

I. SUMMER

Summer, this is our flesh,
The body you let mature ;
If now while the body is fresh
You take it, shall we give
The heart, lest heart endure
The mind's tattering
Blow of greedy claws ?
Shall mind itself still live
If like a hunting king
It falls to the lion's jaws ?

Under the summer's blast
The soul cannot endure
Unless by sleight or fast
It seize or deny its day
To make the eye secure.
Brother-in-arms, remember
The hot wind dries and draws
With circular delay
The flesh, ash from the ember,
Into the summer's jaws.

It was a gentle sun
When, at the June solstice
Green France was overrun
With caterpillar feet.
No head knows where its rest is
Or may lie down with reason
When war's usurping claws
Shall take the heart escheat—
Green field in burning season
To stain the weevil's jaws.

The southern summer dies
Evenly in the fall:
We raise our tired eyes
Into a sky of glass,
Blue, empty, and tall
Without tail or head
Where burn the equal laws
For Balaam and his ass
Above the invalid dead,
Who cannot lift their jaws.

When was it that the summer
(Daylong a liquid light)
And a child, the new-comer,
Bathed in the same green spray,
Could neither guess the night?
The summer had no reason;
Then, like a primal cause
It had its timeless day
Before it kept the season
Of time's engaging jaws.

Two men of our summer world
Descending winding hell
And when their shadows curled
They fearfully confounded

The vast concluding shell:
Stopping, they saw in the narrow
Light a centaur pause
And gaze, then his astounded
Beard, with a notched arrow,
Part back upon his jaws.

II. AUTUMN

It had an autumn smell
And that was how I knew
That I was down a well:
I was no longer young;
My lips were numb and blue
The air was like fine sand
In a butcher's stall
Or pumice to the tongue:
And when I raised my hand
I stood in the empty hall.
The round ceiling was high
And the grey light like shale
Thin, crumbling, and dry:
No rug on the bare floor
Nor any carved detail
To which the eye could glide;
I counted along the wall
Door after closed door
Through which a shade might slide
To the cold and empty hall.

I will leave this house, I said,
There is the autumn weather—
Here, nor living nor dead;
The lights burn in the town
Where men fear together.
Then on the bare floor,
But tiptoe lest I fall,
I walked years down

Towards the front door
At the end of the empty hall.

ALLEN
TATE

The door was false—no key
Or lock, and I was caught
In the house; yet I could see
I had been born to it
For miles of running brought
Me back where I began.
I saw now in the wall
A door open a slit
And a fat grizzled man
Come out into the hall:

As in a moonlit street
Men meeting are too shy
To check their hurried feet
But raise their eyes and squint
As through a needle's eye
Into the faceless gloom,—
My father in a grey shawl
Gave me an unseeing glint
And entered another room!
I stood in the empty hall
And watched them come and go
From one room to another,
Old men, old women—slow,
Familiar; girls, boys;
I saw my downcast mother
Clad in her street-clothes,
Her blue eyes long and small,
Who had no look or voice
For him whose vision froze
Him in the empty hall.

III. WINTER

Goddess sea-born and bright,
Return into the sea

Where eddying twilight
Gathers upon your people—
Cold goddess, hear our plea!
Leave the burnt earth, Venus,
For the drying God above,
Hanged in his windy steeple,
No longer bears for us
The living wound of love.
All the sea gods are dead.
You, Venus, come home
To your salt maidenhead,
The tossed anonymous sea
Under shuddering foam—
Shade for lovers, where
A shark swift as your dove
Shall pace our company
All night to nudge and tear
The livid wound of love.

And now the winter sea:
Within her hollow rind
What sleek facility
Of sea-conceited scop
To plumb the nether mind!
Eternal winters blow
Shivering flakes, and shove
Bodies that wheel and drop—
Cold soot upon the snow
Their livid wound of love.

Beyond the undertow
The grey sea-foliage
Transpires a phospher glow
Into the circular miles:
In the centre of his cage
The pacing animal
Surveys the jungle cove

And slicks his slithering wiles
To turn the venereal awl
In the livid wound of love.

Beyond the undertow
The rigid madrepore
Resists the winter's flow—
Headless, unageing oak
That gives the leaf no more.
Wilfully as I stood
Within the thickest grove
I seized a branch which broke;
I heard the speaking blood
(From the livid wound of love)

Drip down upon my toe:
'We are the men who died
Of self-inflicted woe,
Lovers whose stratagem
Led to their suicide.'
I touched my sanguine hair
And felt it drip above
Their brother who, like them
Was maimed and did not bear
The living wound of love.

IV. SPRING

Irritable spring, infuse
Into the burning breast
Your combustible juice
That as a liquid soul
Shall be the body's guest
Who lights, but cannot stay
To comfort this unease
Which, like a dying coal,

Hastens the cooler day
Of the mother of silences.

Back in my native prime
I saw the orient corn
All space but no time,
Reaching for the sun
Of the land where I was born:
It was a pleasant land
Where even death could please
Us with an ancient pun—
All dying for the hand
Of the mother of silences.

In time of bloody war
Who will know the time?
Is it a new spring star
Within the timing chill,
Talking, or just a mime,
That rises in the blood—
Thin Jack-and-Jilling seas
Without the human will?
Its light is at the flood,
Mother of silences!

It burns us each alone
Whose burning arrogance
Burns up the rolling stone,
This earth—Platonic cave
Of vertiginous chance!
Come, tired Sisyphus,
Cover the cave's egress
Where light reveals the slave,
Who rests when sleeps with us
The mother of silences.

Come, old woman, save
Your sons who have gone down

Into the burning cave:
Come, mother, and lean
At the window with your son
And gaze through its light frame
These fifteen centuries
Upon the shirking scene
Where men, blind, go lame:
Then, mother of silences,

Speak, that we may hear;
Listen, while we confess
That we conceal our fear;
Regard us, while the eye
Discerns by sight or guess
Whether, as sheep foregather
Upon their crooked knees,
We have begun to die;
Whether your kindness, mother,
Is mother of silences.

THE BURIED LAKE

Ego mater pulchrae dilectionis, et timoris,
et agnitionis, et sanctae spei.

Lady of Light, I would admit a dream to you
　　If you would take it in your hand.
　　Will you not let it in a gentle stream

Of living blood? How else may I remand
　　Your light if not as pulse upon your ear?
　　Since I have dreamt this dream at your command,

If it shall bring my edge of darkness near
　　I pray you do not let the edging slough
　　To blind me, but light up my edge of fear.

197

ALLEN
TATE The Way and the way back are long and rough
      Where Myrtle twines with Laurel—single glow
      Of leaf, your own imponderable stuff

Of light in which you set my time to flow.
      In childhood, when I tried to catch each flake
      And hold it to deny the world of snow.

—The night was tepid. I had kept opaque,
      Down deeper than the canyons undersea,
      The sullen spectrum of a buried lake

Nobody saw; not even seen by me.
      And now I pray you mirror my mind styled
      To spring its waters to my memory.

I fumbled all night long, an ageing child
      Fled like a squirrel to a hollow bole
      To play toy soldier, Tiny Tim, and, mild

In death, the Babes with autumn leaves for stole—
      The terror of their sleep I could not spell
      Until your gracing light reduced the toll.

I stumbled all night long on sand and shell
      By a lakeshore where time, unfaced, was dark;
      I grazed with my left foot a pinched hotel;

Where a sick dog coughed out a sickly cark
      To let me in. Inside I saw no man,
      But benches ranged the walls as round a park—

Sputtering gas-jet, ceiling without span
      Where thinning air lay on my cheek like tin;
      But then exulting in my secret plan:

I laid my top hat to one side; my chin
   Was ready; I unsnapped the lyric case;
   I had come there to play my violin.

Erect and sinuous as Valence lace
   Old ladies wore, the bow began to fill
   The shining box—whence came a dreaming face,

Small dancing girl who gave the smell of dill
   In pelts of mordents on a minor third
   From my cadenza for *The Devil's Trill*.

No, no! her quick hand said in a soft surd.
   She locked the fiddle up and was not there.
   I mourned the death of youth without a word.

And could I go where air was not dead air?
   My friend Jack Locke, scholar and gentleman,
   Gazed down upon me with a friendly stare,

Flicking his nose as if about to scan
   My verse; he plucked from his moustache one hair,
   Letting it fall like gravel in a pan,

And went as mist upon the browning air
   Away from the durable lake, the blind hotel,
   Leaving me guilted on a moving stair

Upwards, down which I regularly fell
   Tail backwards, till I caught the music room
   Empty, like a gaol without a cell.

'If I am now alone I may resume
   The grey sonata'—but the box was gone;
   I heard instead three footfalls, a light broom

Dusting the silted air, which now put on—
  Like Pier Francesca sunning a shady wall—
  A stately woman, who in sorrow shone.

I rose; she moved, she glided towards the hall;
  I took her hand but then would set her free,
  'My Love,' I said.—'I'm back to give you all,'

She said, 'my love.' (Under the dogwood tree
  In bloom, where I had held her first beneath
  The coiled black hair, I saw her smile at me.)

I hid the blade within the melic sheath
  And tossed her head; but it was not her head—
  Another's searching skull, whose drying teeth

Crumbled me all night long, and I was dead.
  Down, down below the wave that turned me round,
  Head downwards, where the Head of God had sped

On the third day; where nature had unwound
  And ravelled her green that she had softly laved,—
  The green reviving spray now slowly drowned

Me, since the shuttling eye would not be saved.
  In the tart undersea of slipping night
  The dream whispered while sight within me, caved,

Deprived, poured stinging dark on cold delight,
  And multitudinous whined invisible bees;
  All grace being lost and its considering rite,

Till come to midmost May I bent my knees,
  Santa Lucia! at noon—the prudent shore,
  The lake flashing green fins through amber trees—

And knew I had not read your eye before
   You played it in the flowing scale of glance:
   I had not thought that I could read the score,

Yet how harsh, bitter, and vexed the trance
   Of light—how I resented Lucy's play!
   Better stay dead, better not try the lance

In the living bowl: living we have one way
   For all time in the twin darks where light dies
   To live: forget that you too lost the day

Yet finding it refound it Lucy-guise
   As I, refinding where two shadows meet,
   Took from the burnished umbrage mirroring eyes

Like blue Kentucky on a golden sheet
   Spread out for all my stupor. Lady Coming,
   Lady-not-Going, come Lady come: I greet

You in the sockets of your eyes—humming
   Miles of lightning where (small pastoral scene)
   The fretting pipe is lucent and becoming.

I thought of ways to keep this image green—
   Until the leaf unfold the formal cherry—
   In an off season, when the eye is lean

With an inward gaze upon the wild strawberry,
   Cape jasmine, wild azalea, eglantine—
   All the sad eclogue that will soon be merry;

And knew that nature could not more refine
   What it had given in a looking-glass
   And holds there, after the living body's line

ALLEN
TATE Has moved wherever it must move—wild grass
Inching the earth; and the quicksilver art
Throws back the invisible but lightning mass

To inhabit the room: for I have seen it part
The decanted air, the air close up above
And under you light Lucy, light of heart—

Light choir upon my shoulder, speaking Dove!
The dream is over and the dark expired.
I knew that I had known enduring love.

Leonie Adams

(1899-   )

LIGHT AT EQUINOX

A realm is here of masquing light
When struck rent wood and cornland by
The belled heaven claps the ground.
Husk, seed, pale straw, pale ear the year reposes,
And a thinned frieze of earth rims round
The whey-gleamed wet-as-dimming sky,
And whole trodden floor of light,
Where that slant limb winds with its shadowing closes.

Distant as lustrally the sun
Within that pearl of nimble play
Where traverse with rehearsing tread
Orients of prime to their all-reaping west,
Strangered from every grave glissade
Of blue enduskings or of milky day,
And wan, his silver nimbus on,
Muses his burning sojourn unprofessed.

Past barks mouse-sleek, wattled as serpent skin,
Rare acorn fall, rare squirrel flash.
Beyond, and in a silenced scene,
The wren, gamin wanderer of immense day
Can with luxuriant bendings preen,
Or in his pebble-scoopings plash,
To alarmless Eden flown,
And suddenly, for nothing, flies away.

And all are sole in the estranging day ;
   Forms of all things their candour wear,

Like the undefending dead,
And forth from out that mortal stricture gaze,
Of unperspective radiance shed
Through everywhere horizoned air,
Tasking precising love to say,
For its its dense words, the azuring periphrase.

To her own brink light glides, intent
An unsphering sense to bind
By narrowing measures in.
Sidelong as then up branching March she bade
Stiff buds into the glancing skein,
And the green reel unwind;
Now toward another pole she's leant,
And netherwards for partner draws her shade.

THE FONT IN THE FOREST

Before remembrance we moved here, withheld,
This long reserve beneath what had not been,
Without commencement, late by life that lay,
Offered for anyone and still its own;
Intrusion of its utter forest whose eyes
Abash (nested and laired how deep) which dwell
In their intent. Here on the foreheads dries
The christening freshness of the clear year's front.
And all comes docile to its names, and all
The specious air of creature cannot shield
Unenterable recess. O listener!
Who had not heard the name you listened for,
Beside a font, tongueless, which lichens tinge
With chill frescoings where of day
On day sad afterlight must fall
Changeless upon the falling of a day
Lichens in frond with their dim arms adore.

Ivor Winters

(1899-   )

BY THE ROAD TO THE AIR-BASE

The calloused grass lies hard
Against the cracking plain:
Life is a greyish stain;
The salt-marsh hems my yard.

Dry dikes rise hill on hill:
In sloughs of tidal slime
Shell-fish deposit lime,
Wild sea-fowl creep at will.

The highway, like a beach,
Turns whiter, shadowy, dry:
Loud, pale against the sky,
The bombing planes hold speech.

Yet fruit grows on the trees;
Here scholars pause to speak;
Through gardens bare and Greek,
I hear my neighbour's bees.

A PRAYER FOR MY SON

'Tangled with earth all ways we move.'—JANET LEWIS

Eternal Spirit, you
Whose will maintains the world,
Who thought and made it true;

The honey-suckle curled
Through the arbutus limb,
The leaves that move in air,
Are half akin to him
Whose conscious moving stare
Is drawn, yet stirs by will;
Whose little fingers bend,
Unbend, and then are still,
While the mind seeks an end.
At moments, like a vine,
He clambers through small boughs;
Then poised and half divine,
He waits with lifted brows.
To steep the mind in sense,
Yet never lose the aim,
Will make the world grow dense,
Yet by this way we came.
Earth and mind are not one,
But they are so entwined,
That this, my little son,
May yet one day go blind.
Eternal Spirit, you
Who guided Socrates,
Pity this small and new
Bright soul on hands and knees.

SUMMER NOON: 1941

With visionary care
The mind imagines Hell,
Draws fine the sound of flame
Till one can scarcely tell
The nature, or the name,
Or what the thing is for:
   Past summer bough and cry,

The sky, distended, bare,
Now whispers like a shell
Of the increase of war.
    Thus will man reach an end:
In fear of his own will,
Yet moved where it may tend,
With mind and word grown still.
    The fieldmouse and the hare,
The small snake of the garden,
Whose little muscles harden,
Whose eyes now quickened stare,
Though driven by the sound
—Too small and free to pardon!—
Will repossess this ground.

Janet Lewis

(1899-   )

THE CANDLE FLAME

I feel myself like the flame
Of a candle fanned
By every passionate claim,
Flickering fast,
Or brought to an upright stand
In the curve of a hand.

There is nothing certain, nothing steady
About the mind
That can so alter and wind
Itself in sorrow and mood,
And be ever ready
To change like the leaves in a wood.

And what of our loyalty?
That would turn, alas,
To a flickering vagrancy,
The shadow of grass,
Were it not for the certain, ever-recurring calm
Of the unknown sheltering palm.

Oscar Williams

(1900-   )

THE MIRAGE

I lived a life without love, and saw the being
I loved on every branch; then that bare tree
Stood up with all its branches up, a great harp,
Growing straight out of the ground, and there I saw
A squadron of bright birds clothing the bare limbs;
The music notes sat on the harp; it was all love.

This was the heart inside the starved body;
Love grew images like cactus, and planted roses
On the walls of the mirage, and the garden grew
Shining with perfume and the senses dwindled to dew,
The century was rolled into one formation aloft,
A cloud, like St. Veronica's handkerchief of love.

There I saw the face of the one without whom
I lived, two soft jewels implanted in her face,
Her hair pouring around her face without sound,
And her love for me sprang on her skin like dew,
Pearl-grey as the flower of the brain she lay
Quivering on the soft cushion of the great day.

I heard a roar of buildings at my conscience,
I looked up and saw a wall of windows glowing,
And there my love leaned out of each window,
There she leaned out multiplied like heaven
In that vast wall of lights, every light her face,
Suns of a thousand mornings ranging on one day.

OSCAR
WILLIAMS

And all the machines were running, and yes, great
Was the sound of their running downward and down
Into the blind chutes of their rooted feet,
And all of the windows quivered with my many loves,
Like apples they fell off at one windfall, all,
And I awoke on the starved pavements of no love.

Robert Francis

(1901-   )

WALLS

A passer-by might just as well be blind.
These walls are walls no passer sees behind.
Or wants or needs to want to see behind.
Let the walls hide what they are there to bind.
Out-of-sight they say is out-of-mind.
The walls are cruel and the walls are kind.

SWIMMER

I

Observe how he negotiates his way
With trust and the least violence, making
The stranger friend, the enemy ally.
The depth that could destroy gently supports him.
With water he defends himself from water.
Danger he leans on, rests in. The drowning sea
Is all he has between himself and drowning.

II

What lover ever lay more mutually
With his beloved, his always-reaching arms
Stroking in smooth and powerful caresses?
Some drown in love as in dark water, and some
By love are strongly held as the green sea
Now holds the swimmer. Indolently he turns
To float.—The swimmer floats, the lover sleeps.

ROBERT
FRANCIS

APPLE PEELER

Why the unbroken spiral, Virtuoso,
Like a trick sonnet in one long, versatile sentence?

Is it a pastime merely, this perfection,
For an old man, sharp knife, long night, long winter?

Or do your careful fingers move at the stir
Of unadmitted immemorial magic?

Solitaire. The ticking clock. The apple
Turning, turning as the round earth turns.

Theodore Spencer

(1902-1949)

THE PHOENIX

I

The Sphinx with lion's feet
Comes from the North to greet
At Heliopolis
After ten centuries
The incense-flavoured death,
The holocaust of birth.
To this millennium
Now is also come
The elegant Unicorn
Bearing his graceful horn
Out of the jewelled East;
While slowly from the South
Large gentle Behemoth
Lumbers to watch the fire
Where death will soon expire.
And out of the far West
Comes the last guest,
The enormous, sad-eyed Roc
Folding his huge wings
With feathery shudderings
Like heavy clouds to block
And cramp a desert pool;
Lonely and terrible
He settles to watch the pyre
Of the renascent fire
That will at last redeem
Dead life through flame.

THEO-
DORE
SPENCER

Behold these four creatures
Come to see Nature's
Rare resurrection
From feathers and bone.
Sphinx on the North,
Assured, waiting;
Unicorn on the East,
Aristocratically waiting;
Behemoth on the South,
Motherly waiting;
Dark Roc on the West,
Ominously waiting.

And while they wait in the air that waits for them,
The pyre of incense waits for them and Him.

II

A sudden darkening of the sun
Proclaims the ritual act begun;
A blackening blur against the light—
The aged Phoenix sinks to sight.
His body heavily achieves
The aromatic sticks and leaves;
Almost losing his stiff balance,
He grips with bent rheumatic talons
A sweetly scented log or two
That will his withered force renew,
Totters, and then sinks down to rest
After a thousand years at last
His moulted scabrous ravaged breast
In the hereditary nest.

His father Sun this August day
Shoots down the hot enkindling ray
To light the myrrh and frankincense
As cradle for new innocence.

The flames crackle, sweetly flowering,
The perfumed silken wood devouring,
And, enclosed in flaming petals,
The wrinkled body gently settles
Into the fructifying core
By the caught gazers seen no more:
Until the palisade of flame
Shrivels its roseate diadem
Down to a ruffling coronet
Within whose rim, jauntily set,
Wings akimbo, beak held high,
A whole millennium in his eye,
The fledgling on the whitened coal
Asserts his re-assembled soul,
And, fresh-created paraclete,
Stands on bronze and polished feet;
Then to the sun, the golden sun,
Springs up, his purgatory done,
And on triumphant wings is gone.

But while the ashes fade that fired Him,
Four staring creatures wonder, What of them?

And as night's cooling air
Still finds them silent there,
First the dark bird of ocean
Is troubled into motion,
And to the West returns
As the last glimmer burns.
Back to the waiting South
Lumbers great Behemoth;
And the delicate Unicorn
Back to his Eastern bourn
Steps sadly and slowly;
While in melancholy
The Sphinx walks back
Across her sandy track

THEO-
DORE
SPENCER

To her bleak home of sand,
Piled stones on her right hand.
Oh creatures of man's thought,
Why is man so wrought
That he must make his creatures
Wistful to outlast Nature's
Marriage of flesh and bone?
Like you from South and West,
From North and out of the East,
He yearns to see the death
That flowers to new breath,
The flaming spectacle,
The impossible miracle,
That, like you, occurs
Because man hopes and fears.
But he, like you, goes back
His too-accustomed track,
The rare performance done,
Back, like you, alone.

Wondering whether his mind
That has created you,
And hence created Him,
Was in creation blind,
Or flowering from dead stem,
Flared better than it knew.

Ogden Nash

(1902-   )

PORTRAIT OF THE ARTIST
AS A PREMATURELY OLD MAN

It is common knowledge to every schoolboy and even every
   Bachelor of Arts,
That all sin is divided into two parts.
One kind of sin is called a sin of commission, and that is very
   important,
And it is what you are doing when you are doing something
   you ortant,
And the other kind of sin is just the opposite and is called a
   sin of omission and is equally bad in the eyes of all right-
   thinking people, from Billy Sunday to Buddha,
And it consists of not having done something you shudda.
I might as well give you my opinion of these two kinds of sin
   as long as, in a way, against each other we are pitting them,
And that is, don't bother your head abouts sins of commission because however sinful, they must at least be fun
   or else you wouldn't be committing them.
It is the sin of omission, the second kind of sin,
That lays eggs under your skin.
The way you get really painfully bitten
Is by the insurance you haven't taken out and the checks you
   haven't added up the stubs of and the appointments
   you haven't kept and the bills you haven't paid and the
   letters you haven't written.
Also, about sins of omission there is one particularly
   painful lack of beauty,
Namely, it isn't as though it had been a riotous red letter
   day or night every time you neglected to do your duty;
You didn't get a wicked forbidden thrill

OGDEN   Every time you let a policy lapse or forgot to pay a bill;
 NASH   You didn't slap the lads in the tavern on the back and loudly
         cry Whee,
         Let's all fail to write just one more letter before we go
         home, and this round of unwritten letters is on me.
         No, you never get any fun
         Out of the things you haven't done,
         But they are the things that I do not like to be amid,
         Because the suitable things you didn't do give you a lot more
         trouble than the unsuitable things you did.
         The moral is that it is probably better not to sin at all, but if
         some kind of sin you must be pursuing,
         Well, remember to do it by doing rather than by not doing.

Marya Zaturenska

(1902-   )

THE FALSE SUMMER

It might have been in the heart of a deep forest,
So wide the shade, dense-thicketed where only a pool's
    sound
Strikes;—dancing over stones, with a sound cool and airy,
But it was in a city park, enclosed from the stone street
By an iron gate,
By a phalanx of trees.

We followed a thin stream of rumour, were led to a trail
Of unwinding memory, pounding and low like a moving sea
Till we came to a hot meadow;—then one voice pastoral-
    muted
Pealed through the air like a silver bell and sang like an angel;
It drew rain from the heavens,
Bowed the trembling trees.

By a glint of gold through the trees, we traced the falling
    hair
Of Amaryllis; she who lives in that burning meadow,
Whose voice as cool as a stream calms the false summer,
Who points to a mirage of streams when the soul faints with
    heat,
She who when wheels are turning calls to the pastoral land,
Sings of eternal silence,
Cool grass and tree-arched groves.

Voice of delight and fear to the lost, listening children!
They run for home, they gather their toys, the nursemaids
    call,

And suddenly rivers of blood ran on and on as always,
The nursemaids wept for their old country, green in the
angry sea,
While the heavenly voice kept singing
In the green solitude.

We too remembered the flag at half mast, the crumbling
fortress,
In that old country where we fled to danger
Because the ruins were lovely, because Death wore an
angel's mask,
We saw how the blood-rivers followed, stained the secure
landscape
Even in that rich, round song
The frozen fear, the warning.

We are lost if the iron gate closes, if the intricate thickets
Draw us deep in delightful shade, toward the charmed
singing,
Green song and deep, sharp, pure and steep, clean, green,
Song heard in the opening leaves, the closing flowers,
Do not detain us
Lest you forever claim us.

Amaryllis who sings in the shade till the storm leaps and
gathers,
Till the invaders march through the streets sealing the
fountains,
Poisoning the springs of life, destroying our secret shelters,
Drawing us further from home till we stand on the enemy
street;
And the uneasy charm is broken,
The angel music from a demon's throat.

Merrill Moore

(1903-   )

HE SAID THE FACTS

'That is important. I do not watch the birds':
He said, 'The facts—I only seek for facts—'
He said, 'I do not seek the hidden wish;
That is a fact, if you insist on facts,
But not as people think of them as facts.'

He said: 'Much more important are the acts,
They are the food upon the silver dish.'
He said: 'What is important are the acts;
I mean the way he acts, the way she acts.'

'That is important. I do not watch the birds:
Spinsters do that; I do not count the swords:
Supply sergeants do that; nor list the words:
I leave that to the effing Ph.D's.'

He said: 'All that I do I seek the facts;
The only things that concern me are the acts.'

THEY ALSO STAND...

At midnight, in the garden never planted,
They are unwanted, they were never wanted.

The wanderers in the dark have never come
Upon their use and uses in the kingdom—
The garden with so many in daylight,

MERRILL
MOORE
With the sun to paint their faces white,
Who were wanted, who were always wanted.

Always asking permission to stand there,
Begging the heel of a loaf, something to wear,
Asking for faggots, fuel, asking for food
(They had none of any), all of them stood,
Standing there as if they were rooted there
Begging, and whether it is fair or unfair,
I, standing apart, have seen them standing there.

Edwin Denby

(1903-   )

AIR

Thin air I breathe and birds use for flying
Over and through trees standing breathing in air
Air insects drop through in insect dying
And deer that use it to listen in, share—

Thickens with mist on the lake, or rain
Cuts it with tasteless water and a grey
Day colours it and it is the thin and plain
Air in my mouth the air for miles away.

So close it feeds me each second, everyone's friend
Hugging outside and inside, I can't get rid
Of air, I know it, till the hateful end
When with it I give up the insanely hid

The airless secret I strangle not to share
With all the others as others share the air.

NORTHERN BOULEVARD

The bench, the sewermouth, the hydrant placed
On the street are attractive and foolproof,
Their finish is in republican taste
The expense, on democratic behoof.

People wear the city, the section they use
Like the clothes on their back and their hygiene

And they recognize property as they do news
By when to stay out and where to go in.

Near where a man keeps his Sunday plyers
Or young men play regularly, they place
Next to acts of financial empires
An object as magic as a private face.

No use to distinguish between hope and despair
Anyone's life is greater than his care.

Richard Blackmur

(1904-   )

THE RAPE OF EUROPA

This age it is the same with less remembered.
The first was mounted by a foam-white bull:
Others that came after were less sure
what beast bore God upon them fatally.
Always Europa is a doubting mother /
seeing the torn place struggle to be healed;
while what is born lies shameless in her lap.

This age her whole loveliness lies mauled /
battered and barren from a six-years' bout /
so trod and torn / grossness itself defiled.
Though none could seem to mother her but earth
man monstered God upon her nonetheless.
The muck she lies in mocks the muck of birth
and what is born lies blameless in her lap.

Horror got out of horror may yet be blest
when the great scar of birth begins to scab
and with each change in weather pull and burn
and the wound verge on flow. What bore / tore;
the horror and the glory are the same.
Man's hope the wound / God's memory the scar!
—else what is born lies nameless in her lap.

RICHARD
BLACK-
MUR

SCARABS FOR THE LIVING

I. TOO MUCH FOR ONE: NOT ENOUGH TO GO ROUND

There are too many heart-shaped words for one
to seem enough or two to offer choice;
and yet the heart offers the mind a voice
above all words. Crying its All is None
it is the heart itself that comes undone.

II. IN THE WIND'S EYE

Passionate are palms that clasp in double fist;
compassionate palms lie open to the sky;
on either the dew falls in manna-mist.
Weather is all. The sailor's answering wrist
hauls up / or down / as winds rise / or veer / or die.

III. ON COMMON GROUND

Shambles come ready-made these years / are found
wherever man has stood / or lost / his ground.
So the wide world. It is no otherwise
within the narrow ward where each man lies
apart / his own breathing a shamble-sound.

John Holmes

(1904-   )

WHAT DOES A MAN THINK ABOUT

What does a man think about, working alone all day
Down in the cranberry, fern, and waterlily country?
What does a man know must not happen to him yet
Down in the fog and firefly, dune and old dory country?
Is it his child drowned, is it his boat broken or drifted,
His house hurt by weather, by his own age, by debt?
No. He thinks a boat, wet ditches, weather, the tide
Mean well for him, will be luck, surely make him money,
Down in the bell-buoy, gull, sand, and slow-railroad
    country.
Thinks, somehow all this can give me what I must provide.
What does a man think, driving to get the day's food and
    mail,
Up in the stony-river country, where the evening road is
Pine-cool, steep, old-rotted-moss-log wet, and greener
As the evening valley darkens, cool, colder as light fails
From the granite outcrop down dark trees to the river bed.

Is it a letter more than anything in the world he hopes for?
May be, in the meadow-well, bridge, wild-strawberry
    country.

But a thought of water too much or too little is in his head.
Like speaking of his love too little, or of love too much.

BUCYRUS

A slant-windowed belt-footed enormously long-boomed
Digger, dignified or at least designated as Lima—
That's a place in Peru. What is Lima doing here,
Clawing at Alewife Brook, to lay its water away
In five-foot-round adequate concrete tunnels?

     The alewife, Indian for a sort of herring,
     Maybe meaning aloof, swarmed up this stream.
     They named it who netted a health here.

Bucyrus, a steam-shovel redder than two freight cars,
Hero of tar-paper bunkhouses in the log-boom country;
A big-bucketted up-biter, grunting soft-coal smoke,
He jumbled boulders and raw fill into dinkey-trains
That hauled it through 1910 to build build a dam.

     In the Deerfield East Branch, fish were pike,
     Perch, bass, mostly pike big and criminal,
     The bass flat the other way, a few lost trout.

Bucyrus worked three years to chew up enough Vermont
To dam a river. While he snored in the peeled-pine night
You there could stare at cold air. You could see the
Dead trees out in the water stood up for how hard it is
To kill fish, and get running water under control.

     Bucyrus the whale, grounded and dry-mouthed,
     Tried, and Lima, a Diesel female and nervous,
     Is trying, but the ancient stream runs, water
     Is not to be buried, and the boulders will drift.

THE OVERGROWN BACK YARD

There is a rumour hereabout of summer,
A long green and heavy heat,
By thunder sometimes broken asunder,
And rivers in the street.

But early in the season, with reason,
We began with weapons war
On weeds rising, on the lilac raising
New leaves too far.

Wet makes the grass grow. Sun, we think,
Drinks up the damp. Whet we
Then the hand-sickle against the fickle
Grass, and cut.

The sickle sound, close to the ground,
Is soft. The hooked blade's bevel
Makes fall the grass, that eye may pass
On lawn at level.

That insistent goer, the charging mower,
Hauls back, and pants, and lunges
At tufts and patches. The wheel catches.
But the green changes

From jungle creeping up, to dingle,
To a dell. This clothesyard slope,
From under cover, with this going over,
Begins to take shape.

Richard Eberhardt

(1904-   )

ODE TO THE CHINESE PAPER SNAKE

I

Held on the slightest of bamboo poles,
Suspended from the most voluble of delicate strings,
Heavy in the head, as is proper to subtlety,

His limitation is his slyest and activist, most charm;
Achieves with the least energy the greatest purpose;
Frail in the body, liable to tear, a dissolute.

His eye is horny, he has the feather of imagination
For a fang; his hiss is what you are.
The circuitous pleases him most: circles are endless.

II

The father of a metaphysical principle,
Made in Hong Kong but sold in San Francisco,
The paper snake is foreign to the people of Maine
And has never been seen in the hives of Vienna.

Nearest to stillness his force is most potent.
Thus he adumbrates the meaning of innocence,
Liable in gross action to the unsalvageable and comic;
His least motions manipulate the fiercest evil.

Delicacy is also the mark of civilization
And this is a most uncultured Satanism;
Him no Spengler fingered into exotic play,
Nor divested him of his striking parody.

III

As sex he would be simple, but nothing is simple,
So sexually he bares the fascination of centuries.
He triumphs adept, formally, evident, exquisite.

The ultimate investing philosopher of the future,
A paper snake gives way to none in egoism.
His confidence is masterful and ritualistic,

His is the innate totality of knowledge.
A pertness poses his profundity, deftly expressed,
And it has in it the guile and the smile of the sly.

IV

The pleasantest and the most profound trickery
Is that you can handle as you will this apostle.
It is you who think you control the principle of evil,
It is you who think you invite the charming play of the good.

Nor should we forget forgetfulness, which he induces;
Such rite of resolutions is another of his provinces.
Neither Chinese nor Christian, his characteristic of uni-
    versality

Intrigues as blood, as intellect, as purity, as impurity;
Most inanimate the Chinese snake becomes most animate
Seemingly in the very laughter and sorrow of your being.

V

Aeschylus should have asked of this plaything an answer
As Sophocles spent a lifetime in honouring him;
He was too inward for the Western tone of Shakespeare;
Baudelaire knew him in Paris as a cat.

The heaviness in the Hebrews did not see his dandyism.
Perhaps the greatest effrontery to knowledge
Is that you can manipulate your own fate

231

And as I dandle this fragile, motionable creature
His invitation is the subtle invitation of evil,
The prospect of the Immortal in a paper toy.

VI

And as I think of his perfect, immaterial existence
I am reminded of the deepest human sympathies,
While in his coyness I can make him run.
Inventiveness is his saucy mode, as he spins.

Delectable is the passionate language of the snake,
His motion has in it the stillness of all delectation,
Ancient the sinuousness, instructive the sensibility

For death is in the imagination of that tongue;
But the poison you create in entertaining him
Is swallowed up in waves of orgiastic love.

VII

Or maybe as music as an aftermath
The tantalizing pose always about to be destroyed,
Vagaries of the vigorous, quagmires of the pellucid,
Indices of the contaminations of the realities

You will perceive in fabulous sounds this serpent.
He is present to your skull as in a mirror,
It is the music of your blood you see in his visage.

Delightful is the persuasion of this destroyer,
He is the charming absolute of crumbling fingers,
The dancer, the actor fabulous in the abstract.

VIII

Self-knowledge is the tempter on the stick,
Fair is his eye, ineradicable his logic,
Unquestionable his intention to destroy
Perdurable his ability to maintain!

For you have coiled him up upon himself,
You have looked him in his evil eye,
Adroit, you spurned him into fantasy,

RICHARD
EBER-
HARDT

And you are the pattern of his prophecy!
You are the structure of his massive eye,
And you increase his inviolability.

THE HORSE CHESTNUT TREE

Boys in sporadic but tenacious droves
Come with sticks, as certainly as Autumn,
To assault the great horse chestnut tree.

There is a law governs their lawlessness.
Desire is in them for a shining amulet
And the best are those that are highest up.

They will not pick them easily from the ground.
With shrill arms they fling to the higher branches,
To hurry the work of nature for their pleasure.

I have seen them trooping down the street
Their pockets stuffed with chestnuts shucked, unshucked.
It is only evening keeps them from their wish.

Sometimes I run out in a kind of rage
To chase the boys away; I catch an arm,
Maybe, and laugh to think of being the lawgiver.

I was once such a young sprout myself
And fingered in my pocket the prize and trophy.
But still I moralize upon the day

And see that we, outlaws on God's property,
Fling out imagination beyond the skies
Wishing a tangible good from the unknown.

And likewise death will drive us from the scene
With the great flowering world unbroken yet,
Which we held in idea, a little handful.

Kenneth Rexroth

(1905-   )

MAXIMIAN ELEGY V

(*for Mildred*)

The sky is perfectly clear.
Motionless in the moonlight,
The redwood forest descends
Three thousand feet to the sea,
To the unmoving, silent,
Thick, white fog bank that stretches
Westward to the horizon.
No sound rises from the sea;
And the forest is soundless.
Here in the open windows,
Watching the night together,
I cannot understand what
You murmur, singing sweetly,
Softly, to yourself, in French.
O, lady, you are learned
In your hands that touch me,
In lips that sing obscurely,
In secret, your private songs.
Your face looks white and frozen
In the moonlight, and your eyes
Glitter, rigid and immense.
The illusion of moonlight
Makes you look terror stricken.
And behind you the firelight
Draws back and red frightening
Toppling shadows on the walls.
An airplane crosses, low down,

And fills the landscape with noise
Like an hallucination.
Alive or dead, the stiff heart,
As the hours slide through moonlight,
Squeezes blood and memory.
The fog climbs up the mountain,
And leaves only one star in
The fog bound wood, like an eye
In a tomb. Without warning
Your voice breaks, and your face
Streams with tears, and you stagger
Against me. I do not speak,
But hold you still in my arms.
Finally you say, 'I am not
Weeping for our own troubles
But for the general chaos
Of the world.' I feel you hurling
Away, abandoned on
A parachute of ruin.
A violent shuddering
Overcomes me, as though all
The women like you who had
Ever lived, had stepped across my grave.

MARCUS ARGENTARIUS

Dead, they'll burn you up with electricity,
An interesting experience,
But quite briefly illuminating—
So pour your whisky and kiss my wife or yours,
And I'll reciprocate. Stop fretting your brains.
In Hell the learned sit in long rows saying,
'Some A-s are not B-s, there exists a not B.'
You'll have time to grow wise in their company.

ANTIPATER OF THESSALONICA

KENNETH
REXROTH

Neither war, nor cyclones, nor earthquakes,
Are as terrifying as this oaf,
Who stares, sips water, and remembers
Everything we say.

Stanley Kunitz

(1905-)

THE DAUGHTERS OF THE HORSELEECH

The daughters of the horseleech crying 'Give! Give!'
Implore the young men for the blood of martyrs.
How shall we keep the old senator alive
Unless we satisfy his thirst for cultures?

Entreat the rat, the weasel, and the fox
To forage for a toothless master;
Have mercy, boys, on the monkey in his box;
Dear Judas goat, lead out the sheep to slaughter.

For if the warlock with the gilded claws
Withers away, and of his bones are waters,
Who will transmute our foreheads into brass
And who will keep his five charming daughters?

HE

He runs before the wise men: He
Is moving on the hills like snow.
No gists, no tears, no company
He brings but wind-rise and water-flow.

In meadows of descended day
His motion leans, dividing air:
He takes the unforgiving way
Beneath the apostolic star.

Mary, Mary, call Him Stranger.
Parting the night's long hair, He steals
Within the heart, that humble manger
Where the white, astonished spirit kneels.

STANLEY
KUNITZ

His vertical inflicting pride,
Whose shadow cuts the nib of space,
Bends to this virtue fructified.
But though He kiss the little face

Like rapture breaking on the mind,
The necessary fierce details
Implacably He has designed.
Redemption hangs upon the nails.

END OF SUMMER

An agitation of the air,
A perturbation of the light
Admonished me the unloved year
Would turn on its hinge that night.

I stood in the disenchanted field
Amid the stubble and the stones,
Amazed, while a small worm lisped to me
The song of my marrow-bones.

Blue poured into summer blue,
A hawk broke from his cloudless tower,
The roof of the silo blazed, and I knew
That part of my life was over.

Already the iron door of the north
Clangs open; birds, leaves, snows
Order their populations forth,
And a cruel wind blows.

THE SCOURGE

My heart felt need to die,
Our dusty time had come;
I said, 'Endure the lie,
The waste, the tedium.'

My heart sank to his knees,
Schooled in the tragic style,
But I, being out of heart,
Whipped him another mile,

And not because I cared
To let that actor go,
But only that I feared
His eternal No, No, No.

Beyond the covered bridge
The crooked road turned wild;
He rose at the season's edge,
Passionate and defiled,

Plucking the remnant leaf
Stained with the only good,
While all my children leaped
Out of the glowing wood.

Phyllis McGinley
(1905-   )

COUNTRY CLUB SUNDAY

It is a beauteous morning, calm and free.
    The fairways sparkle. Gleam the shaven grasses.
Mirth fills the locker rooms and, hastily,
    Stewards fetch ice, fresh towels, and extra glasses.

On terraces the sandaled women freshen
    Their lipstick; gather to gossip, poised and cool;
And the shrill adolescent takes possession,
    Plunging and splashing, of the swimming pool.

It is a beauteous morn, opinion grants.
    Nothing remains of last night's Summer Formal
Save palms and streamers and the wifely glance,
    Directed with more watchfulness than normal,
At listless mate who tugs his necktie loose,
Moans, shuns the light, and gulps tomato juice.

PORTRAIT OF A GIRL WITH COMIC BOOK

Thirteen's no age at all. Thirteen is nothing.
It is not wit, or powder on the face,
Or Wednesday matinées, or misses' clothing,
Or intellect, or grace.
Twelve has its tribal customs. But thirteen
Is neither boys in battered cars nor dolls,
Not *Sara Crewe*, or movie magazine,
Or pennants on the walls.

Thirteen keeps diaries and tropical fish
(A month, at most); scorns jumpropes in the spring;
Could not, would fortune grant it, name its wish;
Wants nothing, everything;
Has secrets from itself, friends it despises;
Admits none to the terrors that it feels;
Owns half a hundred masks but no disguises;
And walks upon its heels.

Thirteen's anomalous—not that, not this:
Not folded bud, or wave that laps a shore,
Or moth proverbial from the chrysalis.
Is the one age defeats the metaphor.
Is not a town, like childhood, strongly walled
But easily surrounded; is no city.
Nor, quitted once, can it be quite recalled—
Not even with pity.

Robert Penn Warren

(1905-)

ORIGINAL SIN: A SHORT STORY

Nodding its great head rattling like a gourd,
And locks like seaweed strung on the stinking stone,
The nightmare stumbles past, and you have heard
It fumble your door before it whimpers and is gone:
It acts like the old hound that used to snuffle your door and
    moan.

You thought you had lost it when you left Omaha,
For it seemed connected then with your grandpa, who
Had a wen on his forehead and sat on the veranda
To finger the precious protuberance, as was his habit to do,
Which glinted in sun like rough garnet or the rich old
    brain bulging through.

But you met it in Harvard Yard as the historic steeple
Was confirming the midnight with its hideous racket,
And you wondered how it had come, for it stood so
    imbecile,
With empty hands, humble, and surely nothing in pocket:
Riding the rods, perhaps—or grandpa's will paid the ticket.

You were almost kindly then, in your first homesickness,
As it tortured its stiff face to speak, but scarcely mewed;
Since then you have outlived all your homesickness,
But have met it in many another distempered latitude:
Oh, nothing is lost, ever lost! at last you understood.

But it never came in the quantum glare of sun
To shame you before your friends, and had nothing to do

With your public experience or private reformation:
But it thought no bed too narrow—it stood with lips askew
And shook its great head sadly like the abstract Jew.

Never met you in the lyric arsenical meadow
When children call and your heart goes stone in the bosom;
At the orchard anguish never, nor ovoid horror,
Which is furred like a peach or avid like the delicious plum.
It takes no part in your classic prudence or fondled axiom.

Not there when you exclaimed: 'Hope is betrayed by
Disastrous glory of sea-capes, sun-torment of whitecaps
—There must be a new innocence for us to be stayed by.'
But there it stood, after all the timetables, all the maps,
In the crepuscular clutter of *always*, *always*, or *perhaps*.

You have moved often and rarely left an address,
And hear of the deaths of friends with a sly pleasure,
A sense of cleansing and hope, which blooms from distress;
But it has not died, it comes, its hand childish, unsure,
Clutching the bribe of chocolate or a toy you used to
    treasure.

It tries the lock; you hear, but simply drowse:
There is nothing remarkable in that sound at the door.
Later you hear it wander the dark house
Like a mother who rises at night to seek a childhood picture;
Or it goes to the backyard and stands like an old horse cold
    in the pasture.

PURSUIT

The hunchback on the corner, with gum and shoelaces,
Has his own wisdom and pleasures, and may not be lured
To divulge them to you, for he has merely endured
Your appeal for his sympathy and your kind purchases;

And wears infirmity but as the general who turns
Apart in his famous old greatcoat there on the hill,
At dusk when the rapture and cannonade are still,
To muse withdrawn from the dead and his gorgeous
    subalterns;
Or stares from the thicket of his familiar pain, like a fawn
That meets you a moment, wheels, in imperious innocence
    is gone.

Go to the clinic. Sit in the outer room,
Where like an old possum the snag-nailed hand will hump
On its knee in murderous patience, and the pomp
Of pain swells like the Indies, or a plum.
And there you will stand, as on the Roman hill,
Stunned by each withdrawn gaze and severe shape,
The first barbarian victors stood to gape
At the sacrificial fathers, white-robed, still;
And even the feverish old Jew regards you with authority
Till you feel like one who has come too late, or improperly
    clothed, to a party.

The doctor will take you now. He is burly and clean;
Listening, like lover or worshiper, bends at your heart;
But cannot make out just what it tries to impart;
So smiles; says you simply need a change of scene.
Of scene, of solace: therefore Florida,
Where Ponce de Leon clanked among the lilies,
Where white sails skit on blue and cavort like fillies,
And the shoulder gleams in the moonlit corridor.
A change of love: if love is a groping Godward, though
    blind,
No matter what crevice, cranny, chink, bright in dark, the
    pale tentacle find.

In Florida consider the flamingo,
Its colour passion but its neck a question;
Consider even that girl the other guests shun

ROBERT
PENN
WARREN On beach, at bar, in bed, for she may know
The secret you are seeking, after all;
Or the child you humbly sit by, excited and curly,
That screams on the shore at the sea's sunlit hurlyburly,
Till the mother calls its name, toward nightfall.
Till you sit alone: in the dire meridians, off Ireland, in fury
Of spume-tooth and dawnless sea-heave, salt rimes the
    lookout's devout eye.

Till you sit alone—which is the beginning of error—
Behind you the music and lights of the great hotel:
Solution, perhaps, is public, despair personal,
But history held to your breath clouds like a mirror.
There are many states, and towns in them, and faces,
But meanwhile, the little old lady in black, by the wall,
Who admires all the dancers, and tells you how just last fall
Her husband died in Ohio, and damp mists her glasses;
She blinks and croaks, like a toad or a Norn, in the horrible
    light,
And rattles her crutch, which may put forth a small bloom,
    perhaps white.

Jose Garcia Villa

(1918-   )

BETWEEN GOD'S EYELASHES

Between God's eyelashes I look at you,
Contend with the Lord to love you,
In this house without death I break His skull
I ache, I ache to love you.

I will batter God's skull God's skull God's skull!
I'll batter it till He love you
And out of Him I'll dash I'll dash
In thy coasts, O mortal flesh.

He'll be broken He'll be broken He'll be broken
By my force of love He'll be broken
And when I reach your side O Eve
You'll break me you'll break me you'll break me.

BE BEAUTIFUL

Be beautiful, noble, like the antique ant,
Who bore the storm as he bore the sun,
Wearing neither gown nor helmet,
Though he was archbishop and soldier:
Wore only his own flesh.

Salute characters with gracious dignity,
Though what these are is left to
Your own terms. Exact: the universe is
Not so small but these will be found
Somewhere. Exact: they will be found.

JOSE
GARCIA
VILLA

Speak with great moderation: but think
With great fierceness, burning passion:
Though what the ant thought
No annals reveal, nor his descendants
Break the seal.

Trace the tracelessness of the ant,
Every ant has reached this perfection.
As he comes, so he goes,
Flowing as water flows,
Essential but secret like a rose.

Paul Engle

(1908-   )

CHAMELEON

Chameleon, knowing I am near,
Runs the brown leaf in his brown fear,
Dark as dread and light as light
His swiftness doubles with his fright,
Nimble toe and narrow tongue
Leap with the excited lung,
Long tail astonishes the air
Lashed at nothing, nothing there,

Then jumps to a green leaf that's near
And turns to green in his green fear.
My eyes blink in that altering light
As if his fright were my own fright,
Unwilled and yet aware toe, tongue
Move with my excited lung,
And I am changed in coloured air
By his change, live and sudden there.

I have watched you, slight animal,
On the long stalk of daylight crawl,
Letting the languid noon light run
On hair so burned and quick with sun—
Brown dazzle over you, brown face—
It gave that light a living grace,
And watched you, startled I was near,
Leap up in mingled love and fear.

And let your hand, slight animal,
Over my branching body crawl,

So close did we together run
Touching earth was touching sun,
Change to change and face to face
I moved with greed and you with grace.
Shocked that two could be so near
We feared a love so like a fear.

Theodore Roethke

(1908-   )

MY PAPA'S WALTZ

The whisky on your breath
Could make a small boy dizzy;
But I hung on like death:
Such waltzing was not easy.

We romped until the pans
Slid from the kitchen shelf;
My mother's countenance
Could not unfrown itself.

The hand that held my wrist
Was battered on one knuckle;
At every step you missed
My right ear scraped a buckle.

You beat time on my head
With a palm caked hard by dirt,
Then waltzed me off to bed
Still clinging to your shirt.

ACADEMIC

The stethoscope tells what everyone fears:
You're likely to go on living for years,
With a nurse-maid waddle and a shop-girl simper,
And the style of your prose growing limper and limper.

THE DANCE

Is that dance slowing in the mind of man
That made him think the universe could hum?
The great wheel turns its axle when it can;
I need a place to sing, and dancing-room,
And I have made a promise to my ears
I'll sing and whistle romping with the bears.

For they are all my friends: I saw one slide
Down a steep hillside on a cake of ice,—
Or was that in a book? I think with pride:
A caged bear rarely does the same thing twice
In the same way: O watch his body sway!—
This animal remembering to be gay.

I tried to fling my shadow at the moon,
The while my blood leaped with a wordless song.
Though dancing needs a master, I had none
To teach my toes to listen to my tongue.
But what I learned there, dancing all alone,
Was not the joyless motion of a stone.

I take this cadence from a man named Yeats;
I take it, and I give it back again:
For other tunes and other wanton beats
Have tossed my heart and fiddled through my brain.
Yes, I was dancing-mad, and how
That came to be the bears and Yeats would know.

THE WAKING

I wake to sleep, and take my waking slow.
I feel my fate in what I cannot fear.
I learn by going where I have to go.

We think by feeling. What is there to know?
I hear my being dance from ear to ear.
I wake to sleep, and take my waking slow.

Of those so close beside me, which are you?
God bless the Ground! I shall walk softly there,
And learn by going where I have to go.

Light takes the Tree; but who can tell us how?
The lowly worm climbs up a winding stair;
I wake to sleep, and take my waking slow.

Great Nature has another thing to do
To you and me; so take the lively air,
And, lovely, learn by going where to go.

This shaking keeps me steady. I should know.
What falls away is always. And is near.
I wake to sleep, and take my waking slow.
I learn by going where I have to go.

SONG

Under a southern wind,
The birds and fishes move
North, in a single stream;
The sharp stars swing around;
I get a step beyond
The wind, and there I am;
I'm odd and full of love.

Wisdom, where is it found?—
Those who embrace, believe.
Whatever was, still is,
Says a song tied to a tree.
Below, on the ferny ground,
In rivery air, at ease,
I walk with my true love.

What time's my heart? I care.
I cherish what I have
Had of the temporal:
I am no longer young
But the winds and waters are;
What falls away will fall;
All things bring me to love.

THE SONG

I

I met a ragged man;
He looked beyond me when
I tried to meet his eyes.
What have I done to you?
I cried, and backed away.
Dust in a corner stirred,
And the walls stretched wide.

II

I went running down a road,
In a country of bleak stone,
And shocks of ragged corn;
When I stayed for breath, I lay
With the saxifrage and fern
At the edge of a raw field.
I stared at a fissure of ground
Ringed round with crumbled clay,
The old house of a crab;
I stared, and began to sing.

III

I sang to whatever had been
Down in that watery hole:

I wooed with a low tune;
You could say I was mad.
And a wind woke in my hair,
And the sweat poured from my face,
When I heard, or thought I heard,
Another join my song
With the small voice of a child,
Close, and yet far away.

Mouth upon mouth, we sang,
My lips pressed upon stone.

James Agee

(1908-1955)

DESCRIPTION OF ELYSIUM

There : far, friends : ours : dear dominion :

Whole health resides with peace,
Gladness and never harm,
There not time turning
Nor fear of flower of snow.

Where marbling water slides
No charm may halt of chill,
Air aisling the open acres,
And all the gracious trees.

Spout up their standing fountains
Of wind-beloved green
And the blue conclaved mountains
Are grave guards

Stone and springing field
Wide one tenderness,
The unalterable hour
Smiles deathlessness

No thing is there thinks:
Mind the witherer
Withers on the outward air:
We can not come there.

Sure on this shining night
Of starmade shadows round,

Kindness must watch for me
This side the ground

The late year lies down the north.
All is healed, all is health.
High summer holds the earth.
Hearts all whole.

Sure on this shining night I weep for
    wonder wandering far alone
Of shadows in the stars.

Now thorn bone bare
Silenced with iron the branch's gullet:
Rattling merely on the air
Of hornleaved holly:

The stony mark where sand was by
The water of a nailèd foot:
The berry harder than the beak,
The hole beneath the dead oak root

All is brought quiet
Through the latest throe
Quieted and ready and quiet:
Still not snow

Still thorn bone bare
Iron in the silenced gulley
Rattling only of the air
Through hornleaved holly.

Robert Fitzgerald

(1910-   )

WINDSHIELD

A wet day on the road: the slim blades cutting
Fans of transparency among water jewels;
Distension and rip of high-speed passers-by,
Deaf to the lowly gatherings of the field;
Corn tassels tossed and oak leaves flowing in darkening
Grey rain and western wind.
                                Unplug the lighter
And frown cross-eyed upon that fiery circlet;
There is always something wanting about our hands,
On just-soft cushions lolling or lightly at work
With the slender wheel; and there is something
Perpetually unsaid in what we say—
Our silken exhalations of being friends.
A failure of no consequence?
                                I've dreamed
Of armless men in carnivals, legless men
Knuckling like apes on smoky avenues,
A world's whole host of savage crippled men
Silent but for the single cry: 'Somewhere!'

On each long curve the highway balances
Against our speed with tight terrestrial power,
Conducting to no other place but here;
Here always, the wide alien light of home,
The ever-present wildness of the air—
The nightly dread, say, in cold parishes
Of some tall silvery and unsmiling Father—
A child's wish to do something simply superb.

Winfield Townley Scott
(1910-   )

MR. WHITTIER

It is so much easier to forget than to have been Mr. Whittier.
Though of course no one now remembers him when he was
    young.
A few old ladies who were little girls next door in Amesbury,
Or practically next door, have reminiscences of pears and
    apples
Given them by the famous, tamed, white-bearded saint with
    the
Still inextinguishable dark Hebraic eyes; and
Of course there is the old man—and I for one am grateful—
    who
Recalls the seedy coat, the occasionally not so clean high
    collar,
And that like many another he read his paper by the hour in
    the privy.
Carl Schurz, finding him rained in by the stove at the
    village store,
Thought 'So superior to those about him, and yet so like
    them;' and
His official biographer decided that Mr. Whittier's poetry
    was the kind
'Written first of all for the neighbours.' There are lesser and
    worse.

In any case, here is a city, founded in 1630, present popula-
    tion somewhere about
55,000—has been more in boom times, and has been a lot
    less;—say,

In three hundred years has birthed a couple of hundred
thousand people
And one poet. Not bad. And as proof of the title I shall only
remark
It is easier to leave *Snow-Bound* and a dozen other items in or
out of
The school curriculum than it is to have written them. Try
it and see.

Born where the east wind brought the smell of the ocean
from Plum Island up-River,
At a brookside haunted in the foggy dark of autumn nights
By six little witches in sky-blue capes—Uncle Moses had
seen them;—
Born on a farm to the *Bible*, *Pilgrim's Progress*, a weekly paper,
the Quaker meeting-house,
To hard poverty, obscure, and a few winters of country
school;
To die—though only after there were thirteen for dinner,
and the clock
Suddenly stopped—ancient with fame, with honorary
degrees, and
One hundred thousand dollars all made out of poems—I say
Even this was not easy, though also it is not
What I am talking about, but is really incidental along with
Not liking Walt Whitman and never quite affording
marriage.

Neither, under the circumstances, could it have been easy,
and it was important,
To stand suddenly struck with wonder of old legends in a
young land,
To look up at last and see poetry driving a buckboard
around the bend,
And poetry all the time in the jays screeching at the cats in
the dooryard,

Climbing with the thrush into the August noon out of the
    boy's sight
As he dawdled barefoot through poetry among the welts of
    the goldenrod;
But nothing is hardest which treads on nobody else's toes.

Let us not begrudge Mr. Whittier his white beard, his
    saintliness, his other foibles;
Let us remember him when he was young, not to begrudge
    his rise
As a goddam Abolitionist hated not only in the South,
Hated by manufacturers, politicians, his neighbours, our
    folk, all
Who hate the outspoken radical and know a safer way;
Denounced by the clergy—a serious matter in that time; by
    the good men who
Rotten-egged him in New Hampshire, burned him out in
    Pennsylvania,
Jailed those who read him, and twenty years later im-
    mortally froze
With Webster on whom he turned his scorn of compromise.
It is so much easier to forget than to have been Mr.
    Whittier.
He put the names of our places into his poems and he
    honoured us with himself;
And is for us but not altogether, because larger than us.
When he was an old man, the Negroes came to him free to
    come and sang to him
'The Lord bless thee and keep thee;
The Lord make his face to shine upon thee and be gracious
    unto thee;
The Lord lift up his countenance upon thee, and give thee
    peace.'
—No more begrudge their freedom than his tears.

WIN-
FIELD
TOWNLEY
SCOTT

Josephine Miles

(1911-   )

FORECAST

All our stones like as much sun as possible.
Along their joints run both solar access and decline
In equal splendour, like a mica chipping
At every beat, being sun responsible.

How much sun then do you think is due them?
Or could say, how much sun do you think they are apt to
      have?
It has misted at their roots for some days now,
The grey glamour addressing itself to them.

I should think possible that it go on misting likewise
A good way into next year, or time as they have it,
A regular cool season every day for our stones.
Not a streak that low of any sun or longed surprise.

THE SYMPATHIZERS

To this man, to his boned shoulders
Came the descent of pain.
All kinds
Cruel, blind, dear, horrid, hallowed,
Rained, again, again.

To this small white blind boned face
Wherever it was
Descended

The blows of pain, it took as it were blinded,
As it were made for this.

We were there. We uneasy
Did not know if it were.
Knew neither
The reason nor the man nor whether
To share, or to beware.

Kenneth Patchen

(1911-   )

THE CONSTANT BRIDEGROOMS

Far down the purple wood
Coats of a company
Of silent soldiers
Flap idly in the wind

There they have stood

Since early day
Faces turned incuriously to the sound
Of the dry rustling
Of leaves in the wind

No command has reached

Them there
All silent have they stood
As
Though they were asleep
Now night darkens their coats
Far away
Their names are spoken

Somewhere at world's end

THE EVERLASTING CONTENDERS

KENNETH
PATCHEN

Of the beast . . . an angel
Creatures of the earth
It is good
Any who praise not grandly

O but they should

But they should
Death waits for everything that lives
Beast of the wood
Grim beast of the wood

Who praise not grandly

Should should
Heart weeps for all things
Here
And is greatly comforted
For heart is the angel
Of all
Who praise not grandly

But wish they could

Elizabeth Bishop

(1911-   )

FROM THE COUNTRY TO THE CITY

The long, long legs,
league-boots of land, that carry the city nowhere,
    nowhere; the lines
that we drive on (satin-stripes on harlequin's
    trousers, tights);
his tough trunk dressed in tatters, scribbled over with
    nonsensical signs;
his shadowy, tall dunce-cap; and, best of all his
    shows and sights,
his brain appears, throned in 'fantastic triumph',
    and shines through his hat
with jeweled works at work at intermeshing crowns,
    lame with lights.
As we approach, wickedest clown, your heart and head,
    we can see that
glittering arrangement of your brain consists, now,
    of mermaid-like,
seated, ravishing sirens, each waving her hand-mirror;
    and we start at
series of slight disturbances up in the telephone wires
    on the turnpike.
Flocks of short, shining wires seem to be flying sidewise.
    Are they birds?
They flash again. No. They are vibrations of the tuning-fork
    you hold and strike
against the mirror-frames, then draw for miles, your dreams,
    out countrywards.
We bring a message from the long black length of body:
    'Subside,' it begs and begs.

ROOSTERS

ELIZA-
BETH
BISHOP

At four o'clock
in the gun-metal blue dark
we hear the first crow of the first cock

just below
the gun-metal blue window
and immediately there is an echo

off in the distance,
then one from the back-yard fence,
then one, with horrible insistence,

grates like a wet match
from the broccoli patch,
flares, and all over town begins to catch.

Cries galore
come from the water-closet door,
from the dropping-plastered hen-house floor,

where in the blue blurr
their rustling wives admire,
the roosters brace their cruel feet and glare

with stupid eyes
while from their beaks there rise
the uncontrolled, traditional cries.

Deep from protruding chests
in green-gold medals dressed,
planned to command and terrorize the rest,

the many wives
who lead hens' lives
of being courted and despised;

deep from raw throats
a senseless order floats
all over town. A rooster gloats

over our beds
from rusty iron sheds
and fences made from old bed-steads,

over our churches
where the tin rooster perches,
over our little wooden northern houses,

making sallies
from all the muddy alleys,
marking out maps like Rand MacNally's:

glass-headed pins,
oil-golds and copper-greens,
anthracite blues, alizarins,

each one an active
displacement in perspective;
each screaming, 'This is where I live!'

Each screaming
'Get up! Stop dreaming!'
Roosters, what are you projecting?

You, whom the Greeks elected
to shoot at on a post, who struggled
when sacrificed, you whom they labelled

'Very combative . . .'
what right have you to give
commands, and tell us how to live,

cry 'Here!' and 'Here!'
and wake us here where are
unwanted love, conceit, and war?

The crown of red
set on your little head
is charged with all your fighting-blood.

Yes, that excrescence
makes a most virile presence,
plus all that vulgar beauty of iridescence.

Now in mid-air
by twos they fight each other.
Down comes a first flame-feather,

and one is flying,
with raging heroism defying
even the sensation of dying.

And one has fallen,
but still above the town
his torn-out, bloodied feathers drift down;

and what he sung
no matter. He is flung
on the grey ash-heap, lies in dung

with his dead wives
with open, bloody eyes,
while those metallic feathers oxidize.

.   .   .   .   .

St. Peter's sin
was worse than that of Magdalen
whose sin was of the flesh alone;

of spirit, Peter's,
falling, beneath the flares,
among the 'servants and officers'.

Old holy sculpture
could set it all together
in one small scene, past and future:

Christ stands amazed,
Peter, two fingers raised
to surprised lips, both as if dazed.

But in between
a little cock is seen
carved on a dim column in the travertine,

explained by *Gallus Canit*;
Flet Petrus underneath it.
There is inescapable hope, the pivot;

yes, and there Peter's tears
run down our chanticleer's
sides and gem his spurs.

Tear-encrusted thick
as a medieval relic
he waits. Poor Peter, heart-sick,

still cannot guess
those cock-a-doodles yet might bless,
his dreadful rooster come to mean forgiveness,

a new weathervane
on basilica and barn,
and that outside the Lateran

there would always be
a bronze cock on a porphyry
pillar so the people and the Pope might see

ELIZA-
BETH
BISHOP

that even the Prince
of the Apostles long since
had been forgiven, and to convince

all the assembly
that 'Deny deny deny',
is not all the roosters cry.

In the morning
a lowlight is floating
in the back-yard, and gilding

from underneath
the broccoli, leaf by leaf;
how could the night have come to grief?

gilding the tiny
floating swallow's belly
and lines of pink cloud in the sky,

the day's preamble
like wandering lines in marble.
The cocks are now almost inaudible.

The sun climbs in,
following 'to see the end',
faithful as enemy, or friend.

ELIZA-
BETH
BISHOP

Think of the storm roaming the sky uneasily
like a dog looking for a place to sleep in,
listen to it growling.

Think how they must look now, the mangrove keys
lying out there unresponsive to the lightning
in dark, coarse-fibred families,

where occasionally a heron may undo his head,
shake up his feathers, make an uncertain comment
when the surrounding water shines.

Think of the boulevard and the little palm trees
all stuck in rows, suddenly revealed
as fistfuls of limp fish-skeletons.

It is raining there. The boulevard
and its broken sidewalks with weeds in every crack,
are relieved to be wet, the sea to be freshened.

Now the storm goes away again in a series
of small, badly lit battle-scenes,
each in 'Another part of the field'.

Think of someone sleeping in the bottom of a row-boat
tied to a mangrove root or the pile of a bridge;
think of him as uninjured, barely disturbed.

Delmore Schwartz
(1913-   )

THE HEAVY BEAR

The withness of the body—WHITEHEAD

The heavy bear who goes with me,
A manifold honey to smear his face,
Clumsy and lumbering here and there,
The central ton of every place,
The hungry beating brutish one
In love with candy, anger, and sleep,
Crazy factotum, dishevelling all,
Climbs the building, kicks the football,
Boxes his brother in the hate-ridden city.

Breathing at my side, that heavy animal,
That heavy bear who sleeps with me,
Howls in his sleep for a world of sugar,
A sweetness intimate as the water's clasp,
Howls in his sleep because the tight-rope
Trembles and shows the darkness beneath.
—The strutting show-off is terrified,
Dressed in his dress-suit, bulging his pants,
Trembles to think that his quivering meat
Must finally wince to nothing at all.

That inescapable animal walks with me,
Has followed me since the black womb held,
Moves where I move, distorting my gesture,
A caricature, a swollen shadow,
A stupid clown of the spirit's motive,
Perplexes and affronts with his own darkness,

The secret life of belly and bone,
Opaque, too near, my private, yet unknown,
Stretches to embrace the very dear
With whom I would walk without him near,
Touches her grossly, although a word

Would bare my heart and make me clear,
Stumbles, flounders, and strives to be fed
Dragging me with him in his mouthing care,
Amid the hundred million of his kind,
The scrimmage of appetite everywhere.

THE BEAUTIFUL AMERICAN WORD, SURE

The beautiful American word, Sure,
As I have come into a room, and touch
The lamp's button, and the light blooms with such
Certainty where the darkness loomed before,

As I care for what I do not know, and care
Knowing for little she might not have been,
And for how little she would be unseen,
The intercourse of lives miraculous and dear.

Where the light is, and each thing clear,
Separate from all others, standing in its place,
I drink the time and touch whatever's near,

And hope for day when the whole world has that face:
For what assures her present every year?
In dark accidents the mind's sufficient grace.

Karl Shapiro

(1913-)

PARADOX: THE BIRDS

Wrong about birds. I cannot call
That swift, enslaved, mechanical
Come and go, come and go,
Build and feed and mate and grow
       Beautiful.
Beautiful, the poets are wrong
To love you for your turn and wheel and glide and song
    Beast of the wind, wolf of the tree,
    Heart with the gunner's history,
    Rise and fall, rise and fall,
    Heart of the heart I cannot call
       Liberty.
    Liberty, the poets are wrong
To love you for your turn and wheel and glide and song.

Randall Jarrell

(1914-   )

THE LINES

After the centres' naked files, the basic line
Standing outside a building in the cold
Of the late or early darkness, waiting
For meals or mail or salvage, or to wait
To form a line to form a line to form a line;
After the things have learned that they are things,
Used up as things are, pieces of the plain
Flat object-language of a child or states;
After the lines, through trucks, through transports, to the
    lines
Where the things die as though they were not things—
But lie as numbers in the crosses' lines;
After the files that ebb into the rows
Of the white beds of the quiet wards, the lines
Where some are salvaged for their state, but some
Remanded, useless, to the centres' files;
After the naked things, told they are men,
Have lined once more for papers, pensions—suddenly
The lines break up, for good; and for a breath,
The longest of their lives, the men are free.

THE BREATH OF NIGHT

The moon rises. The red cubs rolling
In the ferns by the rotten oak
Stare over a marsh and a meadow
To the farm's white wisp of smoke.

A spark burns, high in heaven.
Deer thread the blossoming rows
Of the old orchard, rabbits
Hop by the well-curb. The cock crows

From the tree by the widow's walk;
Two stars, in the trees to the west,
Are snared, and an owl's soft cry
Runs like a breath through the forest.

Here too, though death is hushed, though joy
Obscures, like night, their wars,
The beings of this world are swept
By the Strife that moves the stars.

THE KNIGHT, DEATH, AND THE DEVIL

Cowhorn-crowned, shockheaded, cornshuck-bearded,
Death is a scarecrow—his death's-head a teetotum
That tilts up toward man confidentially
But trimmed with adders; ringlet-maned, rope-bridled,
The mare he rides crops herbs beside a skull.
He holds up, warning, the crossed cones of time:
Here, narrowing into now, the Past and Future
Are quicksand.
       A hoofed pikeman trots behind.
His pike's claw-hammer mocks—in duplicate, inverted—
The pocked, ribbed, soaring crescent of his horn.
A scapegoat aged into a steer; boar-snouted;
His great limp ears stuck sidelong out in air;
A dewlap bunched at his breast; a ram's-horn wound
Beneath each ear; a spur licked up and out
From the hide of his forehead; bat-winged, but in bone;
His eye a ring inside a ring inside a ring

That leers up, joyless, vile, in meek obscenity—
This is the devil. Flesh to flesh, he bleats
The herd back to the pit of being.

In fluted mail; upon his lance the bush
Of that old fox; a sheep-dog bounding at his stirrup,
In its eyes the cast of faithfulness (our help,
Our foolish help); his dun war-horse pacing
Beneath in strength, in ceremonious magnificence;
His castle—some man's castle—set on every crag:
So, companioned so, the knight moves through this world.
The fiend moos in amity, Death mouths, reminding:
He listens in assurance, has no glance
To spare for them, but looks past steadily
At—at—a man's look completes itself.

The death of his own flesh, set up outside him;
The flesh of his own soul, set up outside him—
Death and the devil, what are these to him?
His being accuses him—and yet his face is firm
In resolution, in absolute persistence;
The folds of smiling do for steadiness;
The face is its own fate—*a man does what he must*—
And the body underneath it says: *I am.*

John Berryman

(1914-   )

from "HOMAGE TO MISTRESS BRADSTREET"

When by me in the dusk my child sits down
I am myself. Simon, if that's loose,
let me wiggle it out.
You'll get a bigger one there, and bite.
How they loft, how their sizes delight and grate.
The proportioned, spiritless poems accumulate.
And they publish them
away in brutish London, for a hollow crown.

Father is not himself. He keeps his bed,
and threw a saffron scum Thursday. God-forsaken words
escaped him raving. Save,
Lord, thy servant zealous & just.
Sam he saw back from Harvard. He did scold
his secting enemies. His stomach is cold
while we drip, while
my baby John breaks out. O far from where he bred!

Bone of moaning: sung Where he has gone
a thousand summers by truth-hallowed souls;
be still. Agh, he is gone!
Where? I know. Beyond the shoal.
Still-all a Christian daughter grinds her teeth
a little. This our land has ghosted with
our dead: I am at home.
Finish, Lord, in me this work thou hast begun.

JOHN
BERRY-
MAN And they tower, whom the pear-tree lured
to let them fall, fierce mornings they reclined
down the brook-bank to the east
fishing for shiners with a crookt pin,
wading, dams massing, well, and Sam's to be
a doctor in Boston. After the divisive sea,
and death's first feast,
and the galled effort on the wilderness endured,

Arminians, and the King bore against us;
of an 'inward light' we hear with horror.
Whose fan is in his hand
and he will throughly purge his floor,
come towards mé. I have what licks the joints
and bites the heart, which winter more appoints.
Iller I, oftener.
Hard at the outset; in the ending thus hard, thus?

Sacred & unutterable Mind
flashing thorough the universe one thought,
I do wait without peace.
In the article of death I budge.
Eat my sore breath, Black Angel. Let me die.
Body a-drain, when will you be dry
and countenance my speed
to Heaven's springs? lest stricter writhings have me declined.

'What are those pictures in the air at night,
Mother?' Mercy did ask. Space charged with faces
day & night! I place
a goatskin's fetor, and sweat: fold me
in savoury arms. Something is shaking, wrong.
He smells the musket and lifts it. It is long.
It points at my heart.
Missed he must have. In the gross storm of sunlight

I sniff a fire burning without outlet,
consuming acrid its own smoke. It's me.

Ruined laughter sounds
outside. Ah but I waken, free.
And so I am about again. I hagged
a fury at the short maid, whom tongues tagged,
and I am sorry. Once
less I was anxious when more passioned to upset

the mansion & the garden & the beauty of God.
Insectile unreflective busyness
blunts & does amend.
Hangnails, piles, fibs, life's also.
But we are that from which draws back a thumb.
The seasons stream and, somehow, I am become
an old woman. It's so:
I look. I bear to look. Strokes once more his rod.

My window gives on the graves, in our great new house
(how many burned?) upstairs, among the elms.
I lie, & endure, & wonder.
A haze slips sometimes over my dreams
and holiness on horses' bells shall stand.
Wandering pacemaker, unsteadying friend,
in a redskin calm I wait:
beat when you will our end. Sinkings & droopings drowse.

They say thro' the fading winter Dorothy fails,
my second, who than I bore one more, nine;
and I see her inearthed. I linger.
Seaborn she wed knelt before Simon;
Simon I, and linger. Black-yellow seething, vast
it lies fròm me, mine: all they look aghast.
It will be a glorious arm.
Docile I watch. My wreckt chest hurts when Simon pales.

In the yellowing days your faces wholly fail,
at Fall's onset. Solemn voices fade.
I feel no coverlet.

JOHN
BERRY-
MAN Light notes leap, a beckon, swaying
the tilted sickening ear within. I'll—I'll—
I am closed & coming. Somewhere! I defile
wide as a cloud, in a cloud,
unfit, desirous, glad—even the singings veil—

—You are not ready? You are ready. Pass,
as shadow gathers shadow in the welling night.
Fireflies of childhood torch
you down. We commit our sister down.
One candle mourn by, which a lover gave,
the use's edge and order of her grave.
Quiet? Moisture shoots.
Hungry throngs collect. They sword into the carcass.

Headstones stagger under great draughts of time
after heads pass out, and their world must reel
speechless, blind in the end
about its chilling star: thrift tuft,
whin cushion—nothing. Already with the wounded flying
dark air fills, I am a closet of secrets dying,
races murder, foxholes hold men,
reactor piles wage slow upon the wet brain rime.

I must pretend to leave you. Only you draw off
a benevolent phantom. I say you seem to me
drowned towns off England,
featureless as those myriads
who what bequeathed save fire-ash, fossils, burled
in the open river-drifts of the Old World?
Simon lived on for years.
I renounce not even ragged glances, small teeth, nothing,

O all your ages at the mercy of my loves
together lie at once, forever or
so long as I happen.
In the rain of pain & departure, still

Love has no body and presides the sun,
and elfs from silence melody. I run.
Hover, utter, still,
a sourcing whom my lost candle like the firefly loves.

JOHN
BERRY-
MAN

Thomas Merton

(1915-   )

AN ARGUMENT—
OF THE PASSION OF CHRIST

And what one of you, by taking thought, can add to his stature one cubit?—St. Matthew, vi, 27

I

The furious prisoner of the womb,
Rebellious, in the jaws of life,
Learns, from the mother's conscious flesh,
The secret laws of blood and strife.

The demon raging at the breast,
Arrayed in cries, and crowned with tears,
Has sucked the magics of the east,
The doubts of the philosophers.

In the red straits of his arteries,
Love runs, lost and ravening;
Nothingness feeds upon itself
And swells up to a mighty king!

Wit walks out, in envy's mask;
Love will hide, and be a lecher.
Adultery, by taking thought,
Adds a cubit to his stature,

Until we scan the wastes of death,
And wind blows through our cage of bones;
Sight leaves the sockets of the skull,
And love runs mad among the stones!

The worm that watched within the womb
Was standing guard at Jesus' tomb,
And my first angry, infant breath
Stood wakeful, lest He rise from death.
My adolescence, like the wolf,
Fled to the edges of the gulf
And searched the ruins of the night
To hide from Calvary's iron light:
But in the burning jaws of day
I saw the barren Judas Tree;
For, to the caverns of my pride
Judas had come, and there was paid!

III

Seeds of the three hours' agony
Fell on good earth, and grew from me,
And, cherished by my sleepless cares
Flowered with God's Blood, and Mary's tears.
My curious love found its reward
When Love was scourged in Pilate's yard:
Here was the work my hands had made:
A thorny crown, to cut His head.
The growth of thoughts that made me great
Lay on His cross, and were its weight;
And my desires lay, turned to stones,
And where He fell, cut to the bone.
The sharpnesses of my delight
Were spikes run through His hands and feet,
And from the sweetness of my will
Their sponge drew vinegar and gall.

IV

The cry that rent the temple veil
And split the earth as deep as hell
And echoed through the universe,

Sounds, in bombardments, down to us.
There is no ear that has not heard
The deathless cry of murdered God:
No eye that has not looked upon
The lance of the crucifixion:
And yet that cry beats at the ears
Of old, deaf-mute interpreters,
Whose querulous and feeble cries
Drown stronger voices, and whose eyes
Will let no light of lances in:
They still will clamour for a sign!

FIGURE FOR AN APOCALYPSE

Landscape: Beast
Yonder, by the eastward sea
Where smoke melts in a saucer of extinguished cities,
The last men stand, in delegations,
Waiting to see the seven-headed business
Promised us, from those unpublished deeps:
Waiting to see those horns and diadems
And hear the seven voices of the final blasphemy.

And westward, where the other waters are as slick as silk
And slide, in the grey evening, with uncertain lights,
(Screened by the smoke of the extinguished studios)
The last men wait to see the seven-headed thing.
They stand around the radios
Wearing their regalia on their thin excited breasts,
Waving the signals of their masonry.
What will happen, when they see those heads, those horns
Dishevel the flickering sea?
How will they bare their foreheads, and put forth their
        hands
And wince with the last indelible brand,
And wear the dolour of that animal's number,
And evermore be burned with her disgusting name?

Inland, in the lazy distance, where a dozen planes still play THOMAS
MERTON
As loud as horseflies, round the ruins of an average town,
A blue-green medium dragon, swimming in the river,
Emerges from the muddy waters, comes to romp awhile
    upon the land.
She rises on the pathless shore,
And goes to roll in the ashes of the ravaged country.
But no man turns to see and be surprised
Where those grey flanks flash palely in the sun.
Who shall gather to see an ordinary dragon, in this day of
    anger,
Or wonder at those scales as usual as sin?

Meanwhile, upon the broken mountains of the south
No one observes the angels passing to and fro:
And no one sees the fire that shoots beneath the hoofs
Of all the white, impatient horses.

And no one hears or fears the music of those blazing swords.

(Northward, northward, what lies there to see?
Who shall recount the terror of those ruined streets?
And who shall dare to look where all the birds with golden
    beaks
Stab at the blue eyes of the murdered saints?)

Peter Viereck

(1916-   )

COUNTER-SERENADE: SHE INVOKES THE AUTUMN INSTANT

Then touch then park; the leaves are stained to lure you.
The leaves are spread on winds they fan before you,
They drained the summer, and their veins prefer you
Dark with the season they are keening for.

Then bring the heavy dying they prefer.
Each painful fruit is hanging heavier.
Why pause when loveliness grows lonelier
And love is just as melting as it looks?
There's but one touch that all the ripeness lacks:
You are the instant; you are waited for.

Then touch the park. The leaves have spread before you
The green they drained, the darkness they prefer.
Come to the leaves, reach out and touch them all:
Bring to the smouldering year, that hovers for you,
The hovering instant love is dawdling for.

There's not one blade that does not long to fall.

Samuel French Morse

(1916-   )

THE TRACK INTO THE SWAMP

This is the place, as wild as summer snow.
A few square miles of land
Locked in the township where our father lived
Are strange and unexplored.
The idle traffic
Moving north a mile away
Is more familiar than the silt
This coastal stream brings down;
But we have wondered, late in the spring,
How far the river overflowed
Behind the ruined dam.

We know there has been traffic here:
Someone, thirty years ago,
Cleared out a track as far as this.
He must have thought
There was a fortune in the river-sand;
He bound the cedar ties
On something less than rock
And learned the road he had spent a summer on
Was treacherous and vain.
It ends, a narrow path,
In scrub and shadow, farther down.

But if we are more curious than some,
Or have more time,
What was the summer journey he began?
The cedar stands;

And he could see the river from the road,
Or calculate how high it rose in spring
By going to the dam.
What was he looking for, if anything?

He took the longest way to learn
What sedge and grasses thrust
From crumbling ice the glacier left;
Where sundew, like a burning-glass,
Lies open to the light.
Whatever was apparent here
He must have seen,
Though deeper in the swamp, perhaps some trace
Of time before the Pleistocene still shows.
What conscious aim he had
Remains as secret as our own,—
But surely science understands
How deep the inhuman mystery goes;
The wilderness it comprehends
It can explain, like summer snow.

Howard Griffin

(1916-   )

SUPPOSE IN PERFECT REASON

Suppose in perfect reason
you want to die, you want earnestly
knowing for years the meaning,
you want above all to die—
recall the eager, the blonde
beavers who died in shelterhalves
of steel or ground like coral
to reefs where there was no choice.
Life defines the power to choose
and when you cut the thread
you are chosen, you become
a total, a togetherness.
More difficult to go on
bowlining silk-end
to end with awkward hand.
If for any cause you want to die
recall the dead who wanted simply
to live and who had every reason
to go on yet who died
for no accurate reason that you
could name. The pure line
is never poetry
but in walking down the street
to the store.—Wrong or right
they could not be colder dead
whatever side of the fence
the beast is. They eat
out of our mouths, they gaze
through our eyes that look

HOWARD
GRIFFIN

at a plant. If for any cause
you want profoundly to die,
remember the dead. Re-
collect the dead.
Recall the finished dead.

Robert Lowell

(1917-   )

THE DRUNKEN FISHERMAN

Wallowing in this bloody sty,
I cast for fish that pleased my eye
(Truly Jehovah's bow suspends
No pots of gold to weight its ends);
Only the blood-mouthed rainbow trout
Rose to my bait. They flopped about
My canvas creel until the moth
Corrupted its unstable cloth.

A calendar to tell the day;
A handkerchief to wave away
The gnats; a couch unstuffed with storm
Pouching a bottle in one arm;
A whisky bottle full of worms;
And bedroom slacks: are these fit terms
To mete the worm whose molten rage
Boils in the belly of old age?

Once fishing was a rabbit's foot—
O wind blow cold, O wind blow hot,
Let suns stay in or suns step out:
Life danced a jig on the sperm-whale's spout—
The fisher's fluent and obscene
Catches kept his conscience clean.
Children, the raging memory drools
Over the glory of past pools.

Now the hot river, ebbing, hauls
Its bloody waters into holes;

A grain of sand inside my shoe
Mimics the moon that might undo
Man and Creation too; remorse
Stinking, has puddled up its source;
Here tantrums thrash to a whale's rage.
This is the pot-hole of old age.

Is there no way to cast my hook
Out of this dynamited brook?
The Fisher's sons must cast about
When shallow waters peter out.
I will catch Christ with a greased worm,
And when the Prince of Darkness stalks
My bloodstream to its Stygian term . . .
On water the Man-Fisher walks.

AS A PLANE TREE BY THE WATER

Darkness has called to darkness, and disgrace
Elbows about our windows in this planned
Babel of Boston where our money talks
And multiplies the darkness of a land
Of preparation where the Virgin walks
And roses spiral her enamelled face
Or fall to splinters on unwatered streets.
Our Lady of Babylon, go by, go by,
I was once the apple of your eye;
Flies, flies are on the plane tree, on the streets.

The flies, the flies, the flies of Babylon
Buzz in my ear-drums while the devil's long
Dirge of the people detonates the hour
For floating cities where his golden tongue
Enchants the masons of the Babel Tower
To raise tomorrow's city to the sun

That never sets upon these hell-fire streets
Of Boston, where the sunlight is a sword
Striking at the withholder of the Lord:
Flies, flies are on the plane tree, on the streets.

Flies strike the miraculous waters of the iced
Atlantic and the eyes of Bernadette
Who saw Our Lady standing in the cave
At Massabielle, saw her so squarely that
Her vision put out reason's eyes. The grave
Is open-mouthed and swallowed up in Christ.
O walls of Jericho! And all the streets
To our Atlantic wall are singing: 'Sing,
Sing for the resurrection of the King.'
Flies, flies are on the plane tree, on the streets.

FALLING ASLEEP OVER THE AENEID

*An old man in Concord forgets to go to morning service. He falls
asleep, while reading Vergil, and dreams that he is Aeneas at the
funeral of Pallas, an Italian prince.*

The sun is blue and scarlet on my page,
And *yuck-a, yuck-a, yuck-a, yuck-a*, rage
The yellowhammers mating. Yellow fire
Blankets the captives dancing on their pyre,
And the scorched lictor screams and drops his rod.
Trojans are singing to their drunken God,
Ares. Their helmets catch on fire. Their files
Clank by the body of my comrade—miles
Of filings! Now the scythe-wheeled chariot rolls
Before their lances long as vaulting poles,
And I stand up and heil the thousand men,
Who carry Pallas to the bird-priest. Then
The bird-priest groans, and as his birds foretold,
I greet the body, lip to lip. I hold

The sword that Dido used. It tries to speak,
A bird with Dido's sworded breast. Its beak
Clangs and ejaculates the Punic word
I hear the bird-priest chirping like a bird.
I groan a little. 'Who am I, and why?'
It asks, a boy's face, though its arrow-eye
Is working from its socket. 'Brother, try,
O Child of Aphrodite, try to die:
To die is life.' His harlots hang his bed
With feathers of his long-tailed birds. His head
Is yawning like a person. The plumes blow;
The beard and eyebrows ruffle. Face of snow,
You are the flower that country girls have caught,
A wild bee-pillaged honey-suckle brought
To the returning bridegroom—the design
Has not yet left it, and the petals shine;
The earth, its mother, has, at last, no help:
It is itself. The broken-winded yelp
Of my Phoenician hounds, that fills the brush
With snapping twigs and flying, cannot flush
The ghost of Pallas. But I take his pall,
Stiff with its gold and purple, and recall
How Dido hugged it to her, while she toiled,
Laughing—her golden threads, a serpent coiled
In cypress. Now I lay it like a sheet;
It clinks and settles down upon his feet,
The careless yellow hair that seemed to burn
Beforehand. Left foot, right foot—as they turn,
More pyres are rising: armoured horses, bronze,
And gagged Italians, who must file by ones
Across the bitter river, when my thumb
Tightens into their wind-pipes. The beaks drum;
Their headman's cow-horned death's-head bites its tongue,
And stiffens, as it eyes the hero slung
Inside his feathered hammock on the crossed
Staves of the eagles that we winged. Our cost
Is nothing to the lovers, whoring Mars

And Venus, father's lover. Now his car's
Plumage is ready, and my marshals fetch
His squire, Acoetes, white with age, to hitch
Aethon, the hero's charger, and its ears
Prick, and it steps and steps, and stately tears
Lather its teeth; and then the harlots bring
The hero's charms and baton—but the King,
Vain-glorious Turnus, carried off the rest.
'I was myself, but Ares thought it best
The way it happened.' At the end of time,
He sets his spear, as my descendants climb
The knees of Father Time, his beard of scalps,
His scythe, the arc of steel that crowns the Alps.
The elephants of Carthage hold those snows,
Turms of Numidian horse unsling their bows,
The flaming turkey-feathered arrows swarm
Beyond the Alps. 'Pallas,' I raise my arm
And shout, 'Brother, eternal health. Farewell
Forever.' Church is over, and its bell
Frightens the yellowhammers, as I wake
And watch the whitecaps wrinkle up the lake.
Mother's great-aunt, who died when I was eight,
Stands by our parlour sabre. 'Boy, it's late.
Vergil must keep the Sabbath.' Eighty years!
It all comes back. My Uncle Charles appears.
Blue-capped and bird-like. Phillips Brooks and Grant
Are frowning at his coffin, and my aunt,
Hearing his coloured volunteers parade
Through Concord, laughs, and tells her English maid
To clip his yellow nostril hairs, and fold
His colours on him . . . It is I, I hold
His sword to keep from falling, for the dust
On the stuffed birds is breathless, for the bust
Of young Augustus weighs on Vergil's shelf:
It scowls into my glasses at itself.

Walker Gibson

(1919-   )

DAVID

Master of metaphor, at three
He's learned the language of mirage—
Sees dump trucks climbing every tree;
The sky, he says, is their garage.

And like a derrick, drops his head;
Contrives his airplane arms like flaps;
Mother and father sleep like dead;
Behind the barn the dead cat naps.

This is no simple world. To him
Man is machine, machine is man,
And the corpse talks, the lilies swim.
Of course, we tell him what we can.

Robert Duncan

(1919-   )

THE REAPER

Created by the poet to sing my song,
or created by my song to sing.

The source of the song must die away.

All day the night of music hovers
In the fir-tree, swims and glitters.
O touch me not to song
I desire to be forever mute with my first Lord.

The source of the song will die away.

Glorious is the hot sun.
The reaper in his youth cuts down the living grain.
We see the glitter of his hot curved scythe.
His weary labours cut us down
while yet we live.

The source of the song will die away.

Sweep not upon the strings of my dark lyre,
my body, music; make mute
the tree within my heart, for I desire
to come unto my Lord unsung: the Tomb
of Muses in the marble of the flesh
is like a monument of song.

The source of the song will die away.

All night the pestilential reaper slays.
We fall away beneath his blade.
Our youth is daily harvested like wheat
from fields of our first Lord

The source of the song will die away.

But see, glorious is the hot sun.
The Reaper cuts my hot youth down.
He cuts me down from my first Lord
while yet I live.

The source of the song will die away.

HERO SONG

There was no repose.

We think of them
at the boundaries
crows of a carrion world
natural to the cold
driven forward, forced back.

caw, caw, caw.

He was a light in our restlessness,
shedding no light
but luminous in himself—
on electric cloud,
then, embodied,
a torso foreign to our despair.

Death does not come down upon us.
We wait for him.

For the great carnal striker
to level our pride.

Brides to our future,
we hear the crows cawing.

    Away! Away!

Fear is mysterious
to instil resistance.

We resist at the boundaries of the day
the first light we have seen

the incandescence of the dead.

Love, he said,
    will eat away the Empire
    until chaos remains.

James Broughton

(1920-   )

THE LIGHTHOUSE KEEPER'S OFFSPRING

Storms once hurled my howls about,
but now no traumas worry me.
I the skiff that hugged safe harbour
find no harbour save the sea.

And there is where I'll choose to bed,
stretching out on rolling tide.
There my boat shall aim its sailing,
there will I like Christmas glide.

Gods unknown, O god of racing,
grace me fleets to steer my own.
If free I can, if me I can,
such as this my bold will go:

Straight across the world's old sorrow,
lightly rigged for shipshape seas,
and all of earth's dry murder thrown
overboard with ease.

GENESIS OF VOWELS

A is to begin with, and A began with Adam.
E is to proceed with, and Eve was her name.
I is what they ended with, and I of course is me.
O is how they did it, O over O and over.
U is what undid them, underneath the game.

For Y was added to the act.
Adamant is Y.
Even crawling inside O
it yowls at U and I.

JAMES
BROUGH-
TON

Chester Kallman

(1921-   )

NIGHTMARE OF A COOK

And the day arrives at last, my friends,
When the breakwater drops like a duck's head
Before your unweanable greed,
As I, pip-squeak and upset,
Your lunch two hours late,
Circle on one shorter leg about the sands,
And you come on, your voices
Merged in a driving whimper, but
How well I know your faces.

For each of you two faces.
One: as I entered, candlelight
Gave up your greasy hands
At once to my greedy sight,
And bluntly your eyes said, *Caught*!
As you dropped all thought of excuses
For killing the Great White Goose.
The other: you came in suddenly, eyes bright,
Eyes sharp as those of one who finds
Confirmed a wished unfaithfulness,
While I sat morbidly among my dead,
The groaning board of isolation spread.

An instant, from a bird's eye, spread
Lie sea and beach below me, but
I am where I am and you, a sea of hands,
A sea of eyes, all mouth, all simplified,
Come on; and you will not be stupefied by spices

Nor compromise with sauces
When you take your time, and even the neat
Scavenger, the feeling snail, will get
Nothing of me, when you are done, my friends.

LITTLE EPITHALAMIUM

Oak, fern, ivy and pine:
What they are, not the sound spoken,
The words only as invocation
Permitting me their presence again.
The bus climbed from the narrow plain,
From the palm-lined shore; on the mountain
Were oak, fern, ivy and pine,
A tang in the air. I was not alone,
I was not alone. And later when
We returned, under a sickle moon
The blue broke in a fleece-white ribbon
Along the beach. We came down
Through the mountain air, not a word spoken.
Let me, a moment, have as mine
What is ever, and even in possession,
A blessed, blessing separation
Making one, making one.
I say them in ceremony again:
Oak, fern, ivy and pine.

URBAN HISTORY

We said *We understand*, and for a while
    Perhaps in truth we really founded
        A calm within that wheel
Whereon the flock, in dreams of holy-land,

Are moved by nothing real.
We loved, we nested, saw no evil,
And wakefully to folly blind,
We studied what to feel.

We said *We understand*, to clear a while
A working interval surrounded
By an uncertain wall;
But patiently across the civil sand,
The waves of madness crawl,
And almost as we heard the babble
Afar of that uncertain sound,
We knew what must befall.

We said *We understand*, but even while
We spoke, and speaking hailed a rounded
New world where all was well,
Some dreaming sybil idly bade the wind
Speak Heaven and speak Hell,
A God was born of woman, Virgil
Burrowed the rock, we saw the wound,
Man was redeemed, Rome fell.

We understood it, and a little while
Later were not at all astounded
When Love did what He will.
It is over, we said. *We understand*.
It is not over still:
The wind raves on with tongues that Babel
Failed to define; the sea, unstained,
Haunts what it cannot fill.

Richard Wilbur

(1921-   )

POTATO

for André du Bouchet

An underground grower, blind and a common brown;
Got a misshapen look, it's nudged where it could;
Simple as soil yet crowded as earth with all.

Cut open raw, it loosens a cool clean stench,
Mineral acid seeping from pores of prest meal;
It is like breaching a strangely refreshing tomb:

Therein the taste of first stones, the hands of dead slaves,
Waters men drank in the earliest frightful woods,
Flint-chips, and peat, and the cinders of buried camps.

Scrubbed under faucet water the planet skin
Polishes yellow, but tears to the plain insides;
Parching, the white's blue-hearted like hungry hands.

All of the cold dark kitchens, and war-frozen grey
Evening at window; I remember so many
Peeling potatoes quietly into chipt pails.

'It was potatoes saved us, they kept us alive.'
Then they had something to say akin to praise
For the mean earth-apples, too common to cherish or steal.

Times being hard, the Sikh and the Senegalese,
Hobo and Okie, the body of Jesus the Jew,
Vestigial virtues, are eaten; we shall survive.

What has not lost its savour shall hold us up,
And we are praising what saves us, what fills the need.
(Soon there'll be packets again, with Algerian fruits.)

Oh, it will not bear polish, the ancient potato,
Needn't be nourished by Caesars, will blow anywhere,
Hidden by nature, counted-on, stubborn and blind.

You may have noticed the bush that it pushes to air,
Comical-delicate, sometimes with second-rate flowers
Awkward and milky and beautiful only to hunger.

BEASTS

Beasts in the major freedom
Slumber in peace tonight. The gull on his ledge
Dreams in the guts of himself the moon-plucked waves
below,
And the sunfish leans on a stone, slept
By the lyric water;

In which the spotless feet
Of deer make dulcet splashes, and to which
The ripped mouse, safe in the owl's talon, cries
Concordance. Here there is no such harm
And no such darkness

As the selfsame moon observes
Where, warped in window-glass, it sponsors now
The werewolf's painful change. Turning his head away
On the sweaty bolster, he tries to remember
The mood of manhood,

But lies at last, as always,
Letting it happen, the fierce fur soft to his face,

Hearing with sharper ears the wind's exciting minors,
 The leaves' panic, and the degradation
  Of the heavy streams.

    Meantime, at high windows
  Far from thicket and pad-fall, suitors of excellence
Sigh and turn from their work to construe again the painful
  Beauty of heaven, the lucid moon
    And the risen hunter,

    Making such dreams for men
  As told will break their hearts as always, bringing
Monsters into the city, crows on the public statues,
  Navies fed to the fish in the dark
    Unbridled waters.

BEOWULF

The land was overmuch like scenery,
The flowers attentive, the grass too garrulous green;
In the lake like a dropped kerchief could be seen
The lark's reflection after the lark was gone;
The Roman road lay paved too shiningly
For a road so many men had travelled on.

Also the people were strange, were strangely warm.
The king recalled the father of his guest,
The queen brought mead in a studded cup, the rest
Were kind, but in all was a vagueness and a strain,
Because they lived in a land of daily harm.
And they said the same things again and again.

It was a childish country; and a child,
Grown monstrous, so besieged them in the night
That all their daytimes were a dream of fright

That it would come and own them to the bone.
The hero, to his battle reconciled,
Promised to meet that monster all alone.

So then the people wandered to their sleep
And left him standing in the echoed hall.
They heard the rafters rattle fit to fall,
The child departing with a broken groan,
And found their champion in a rest so deep
His head lay harder sealed than any stone.

The land was overmuch like scenery,
The lake gave up the lark, but now its song
Fell to no ear, the flowers too were wrong,
The day was fresh and pale and swiftly old,
The night put out no smiles upon the sea;
And the people were strange, the people strangely cold.

They gave him horse and harness, helmet and mail,
A jewelled shield, an ancient battle-sword,
Such gifts as are the hero's hard reward
And bid him do again what he has done.
These things he stowed beneath his parting sail,
And wept that he could share them with no son.

He died in his own country a kinless king,
A name heavy with deeds, and mourned as one
Will mourn for the frozen year when it is done.
They buried him next the sea on a thrust of land:
Twelve men rode round his barrow all in a ring,
Singing of him what they could understand.

Dachine Rainer

(1921-   )

DOUBLE RITUAL

for Baby Thérèse and Grandpa Mendel

Death thresholded old man hold
Upon your uncertain lap—here, hold!
Upon your near centuried lap
Your golden child.

And smile your ancient heartworn ache:
There is no place for an old man.

This is the dance of youth and old age,
Kick high!
You wear death in place of the features
We knew. Kick high! Kick high.

Death's intervening face affronts my gaze,
Oh no. This is no place.

Too late: it scarcely seems worth the journey's weight
To bring the child's gaiety for your poor sight.
Dim old man, dear grandpa, homeless and confined,
I grieve years long with an enduring grief

For you, earth ridden, wandering and shackled, in the
         hospital
Of an old age home. There is no place for an old man.

    That she may look upon the earth
    I cast her on, and weep for all the shipwrecks,

All the castaways,
That she may view the sorrow

Of unalterable loneliness
Before her infant mind can penetrate its mysteries,

To inoculate her spirit
Against the dreadful vagaries
Of brutal man, I bring her here,
And for your benedictine touch, your glance, your
winging wishes.

Where there is no place for an old man
There is no place for anyone.

But, there! she moves upon your lap
As though the great wheel on which we all ride
Stirred her, as though wheels, worlds, the moving
years
On centuries leaned upon her tiny thoughtful form

As she sits, gazing out from the bright rim of all the
heavens
Upon the shell of night.

Robert Horan

(1922-   )

LITTLE CITY

Spider, from his flaming sleep,
staggers out into the window frame;
swings out from the red den where he slept
to nest in the gnarled glass.
Fat hero, burnished cannibal
lets down a frail ladder and ties a knot,
sways down to a landing with furry grace.

By noon this corner is a bullet-coloured city
and the exhausted architect
sleeps in his pale wheel,
waits without pity for a gold visitor
or coppery captive, his aerial enemies
spinning headlong down the window to the trap.

The street of string shakes now and announces
a surprised angel in the tunnel of thread.
Spider dances down his wiry heaven to taste the moth.

A little battle begins and the prison trembles.
The round spider hunches like a judge.
The wheel glistens.
But this transparent town that caves in at a breath
is paved with perfect steel.
The victim hangs by his feet, and the spider
circles invisible avenues, weaving a grave.

By evening the web is heavy with monsters,
bright constellation of wasps and bees,

breathless, surrendered.
Bronze skeletons dangle on the wires
and a thin wing flutters.
The medieval city hangs in its stars.

Spider lumbers down the web
and the city stretches with the weight of his walking.
By night we cannot see the flies' faces
and the spider, rocking.

EMBLEMS OF EVENING

Look, sunset's all undone!
Blackbird, no platform to swim from
but pinnacles of pine.
The garden is ribboned with red,
ladders of washing wine

The sun-dial shows one dazzled inch
on its purple wheel.
The statues stand in clots of shadow;
all retreat, scarved and mute,
toward the horizon of the unreal.

Rush, in rare dusk, the crippled moths;
around the woollen light, toss and flow.
There are no stars yet, but rents in cloth
which will later glow,
an intermittent meadow.

The deer in their dewing hovels
fold their legs.
Sleep holds toward them,
and the staring frogs, homes.

(Your eyes behind their lowered lids
travel a blue parabola.
Medallions of the sunken sun
glimmer on your lean shoulder.)

ROBERT
HORAN

Anthony Hecht

(1922-   )

THE PLACE OF PAIN IN THE UNIVERSE

Mixture of chloroform and oil of cloves
Swabbed with a wadded toothpick on the gums
Grants us its peace by slackening the thread
Of rich embroidered nerve spun in the head,
And to the weak and wretched jaw it comes
Lighter than manna and in sweeter loaves.

An old engraving pictures St. Jerome
Studying at his table, where a skull,
Crowned with a candle, streams cold tears of wax
On its bone features for the flesh it lacks,
Yet its white complement of teeth is full
While all its pain runs happily to loam.

Observe there is no easy moral here.
Having received their diet from the skies
The teeth remain, although they cannot bite,
And to perform inspection beyond sight
The empty sockets famish for their eyes,
The pain is lifelike in that waxwork tear.

JAPAN

It was a miniature country once
To my imagination; Home of the Short,
And also the academy of stunts
    Where acrobats are taught

The famous secrets of the trade:
   To cycle in the big parade
While spinning plates upon their parasols,
Or somersaults that do not touch the ground,
      Or tossing seven balls
In Most Celestial Order round and round.

A child's quick sense of the ingenious stamped
All their invention: toys I used to get
At Christmastime, or the peculiar, cramped
      Look of their alphabet.
   Fragile and easily destroyed,
   Those little boats of celluloid
Driven by camphor round the bathroom sink,
And delicate the folded paper prize
      Which, dropped into a drink
Of water, grew up right before your eyes.

Now when we reached them it was with a sense
Sharpened for treachery compounding in their brains
Like mating weasels; our Intelligence
      Said: The Black Dragon reigns
   Secretly under yellow skin,
   Deeper than dyes of atabrine
And deadlier. The War Department said:
Remember you are Americans; forsake
      The wounded and the dead
At your own cost; remember Pearl and Wake.

And yet they bowed us in with ceremony,
Told us what brands of Sake were the best,
Explained their agriculture in a phony
      Dialect of the West,
   Meant vaguely to be understood
   As a shy sign of brotherhood
In the old human bondage to the facts
Of day-to-day existence. And like ants,

Signalling tiny pacts
                With their antennae, they would wave their hands.

At last we came to see them not as glib
Walkers of tightropes, worshippers of carp,
Nor yet a species out of Adam's rib
        Meant to preserve its warp
    In Cain's own image. They had learned
    That their tough eye-born goddess burned
Adoring fingers. They were very poor.
The holy mountain was not moved to speak.
        Wind at the paper door
Offered them snow out of its hollow peak.

Human endeavour clumsily betrays
Humanity. Their excrement served in this;
    For, planting rice in water, they would raise
        Schistosomiasis
        Japonica, that enters through
        The pores into the avenue
And orbit of the blood, where it may foil
The heart and kill, or settle in the brain.
        This fruit of their nightsoil
Thrives in the skull, where it is called insane.

Now the quaint early image of Japan
That was so charming to me as a child
Seems like a bright design upon a fan,
        Of water rushing wild
    On rocks that can be folded up,
    A river which the wrist can stop
With a neat flip, revealing merely sticks
And silk of what had been a fan before,
        And like such clever tricks,
    It shall be buried in excelsior.

ACKNOWLEDGMENTS

For permission to reprint these poems, thanks are due the following poets, their copyright holders, and publishers:

RICHARD BLACKMUR—for his poems from *The Good European* (Cummington Press, 1947).

BRANDT & BRANDT—for "Invocation" from "John Brown's Body" by Stephen Vincent Benét in *Selected Works of Stephen Vincent Benét* (Rinehart & Co.), copyright 1927, 1928 by Stephen Vincent Benét; for poems of E. E. Cummings from *Poems 1923-1954* by E. E. Cummings (Harcourt Brace & Co.), copyright 1925, 1940, 1944, 1950, 1953 by E. E. Cummings; and for poems of Edna St. Vincent Millay from *Collected Lyrics of Edna St. Vincent Millay* (Harper & Bros.), copyright 1923, 1928, 1934 by Edna St. Vincent Millay.

JAMES BROUGHTON—for his poems from *Musical Chairs* (Centaur-Press, 1947).

EDWIN DENBY—for his poems from *In Public, In Private* (J. A. Decker, 1948).

DOUBLEDAY & CO.—for poems of Don Marquis from *Archy's Life of Mehitabel* by Don Marquis, copyright 1933 by Doubleday & Co.; for "Academic" from *Open House* by Theodore Roethke, copyright 1941 by Theodore Roethke; "The Dance" (copyright 1952 by the *Atlantic Monthly* Co.), "Four for Sir John Davies," and "The Waking" from *The Waking, Poems 1933-1953*, copyright 1953 by Theodore Roethke; and "My Papa's

Waltz" from *The Lost Son and Other Poems,* copyright 1942 by Hearst Magazines Inc.

ROBERT DUNCAN—for "The Reaper" from *Medieval Scenes* (Centaur Press, 1950), and "Hero Song."

FARRAR, STRAUS, and CUDAHY—for the poem of John Berryman, an excerpt from *Homage to Mistress Bradstreet,* copyright 1956 by John Berryman.

ROBERT FRANCIS—for "Swimmer" and "Apple Peeler," copyright 1953 by Ballantine Books, Inc.

FUNK & WAGNALLS—for poems of Léonie Adams from *Poems, A Selection* by Léonie Adams, copyright 1954 by Léonie Adams.

HOWARD GRIFFIN—for his poem.

GROVE PRESS—for poems by Chester Kallman from *Storm at Castlefranco,* copyright 1956 by Chester Kallman.

HARCOURT BRACE & CO.—for "The Lines" and "The Breath of Night" from *Losses* by Randall Jarrell, copyright 1948 by Harcourt Brace & Co.; "The Knight, Death, and the Devil" from *The Seven League Crutches* by Randall Jarrell, copyright 1951 by Randall Jarrell; for "The Drunken Fisherman" from *Lord Weary's Castle* by Robert Lowell, copyright 1944, 1946 by Robert Lowell, and "Falling Asleep Over the Aeneid" from *The Mills of the Kavanaughs* by Robert Lowell, copyright 1946, 1947, 1948, 1950, 1951 by Robert Lowell; for poems of Josephine Miles from *Local Measures* by Josephine Miles, copyright 1946 by Josephine Miles; for "Bas-Relief" from *Smoke and Steel* by Carl Sandburg, copyright 1920 by Harcourt Brace & Co., renewed 1948 by Carl Sandburg; for poems of Louis Untermeyer from *Selected Poems and Parodies of Louis Untermeyer*, copyright 1935 by Harcourt Brace & Co.; for "Potato" from *The Beautiful Changes and Other Poems* by Richard Wilbur, copyright 1947 by Richard Wilbur, "Beowulf" from *Ceremony and Other Poems* by Richard Wilbur, copyright 1950 by Richard Wilbur, and "Beasts" from *Things of This World* by Richard Wilbur, copyright 1956 by Richard Wilbur.

HARVARD UNIVERSITY PRESS—for poem of Theodore Spencer from *Poems, 1940-1947* by Theodore Spencer, copyright 1948 by The President and Fellows of Harvard College.

JOHN HOLMES—for his poem "Bucyrus."

HENRY HOLT AND CO.—for poems of Robert Frost from *Complete Poems of Robert Frost*, copyright 1930, 1949 by Henry Holt and Co., 1936, 1948 by Robert Frost; for poems of Samuel Greenberg from *Poems by Samuel Greenberg*, copyright 1947 by Harold Holden and Jack McManis; for "The Daughters of the Horseleech" and "He" from *Passport to the War* by Stanley Kunitz, copyright 1930, 1944 by Stanley Kunitz; for "Personality" from *Chicago Poems* by Carl Sandburg, copyright 1916 by Henry Holt and Co., 1944 by Carl Sandburg, and "Clocks" from *Cornhuskers* by Carl Sandburg, copyright 1918 by Henry Holt and Co., 1946 by Carl Sandburg.

ROBERT HORAN—for "Emblems of Evening."

HOUGHTON MIFFLIN CO.—for poems of Elizabeth Bishop from *North and South* by Elizabeth Bishop (1946); and for poems of Archibald MacLeish from *Collected Poems* by Archibald MacLeish, copyright 1952 by Archibald MacLeish.

BRUCE HUMPHRIES, INC.—for poems of John Wheelright from *Rock and Shell* by John Wheelright, copyright 1933 by Bruce Humphries, Inc.

INDIANA UNIVERSITY PRESS—for the poem by Walker Gibson from *The Reckless Spender* by Walker Gibson.

ALFRED A. KNOPF—for poems of Witter Bynner from *Selected Poems* by Witter Bynner, copyright 1935, 1936 by Alfred A. Knopf, Inc.; for poems of Stephen Crane from *The Collected Poems of Stephen Crane*, copyright 1930 by Alfred A. Knopf, Inc.; for "Vision By Sweetwater" from *Two Gentlemen in Bonds* by John Crowe Ransom, copyright 1927 by Alfred A. Knopf, Inc., and all other poems of John Crowe Ransom from *Selected Poems* by John Crowe Ransom, copyright 1924, 1927, 1945 by Alfred A. Knopf, Inc.; for poems of Wallace Stevens from *The Collected Poems of Wallace Stevens*, copyright 1931, 1942, 1954 by Wallace Stevens; and for poems of Elinor Wylie from *Collected Poems of Elinor Wylie*, copyright 1923, 1932 by Alfred A. Knopf, Inc.

STANLEY KUNITZ—for "End of Summer," copyright 1953 by The New American Library of World Literature, Inc., and "The Scourge," copyright 1954 by *The Hudson Review, Inc.*

LITTLE, BROWN AND CO.—for the poem by Ogden Nash from *Many Long Years Ago* by Ogden Nash, copyright 1935 by Ogden Nash.

LIVERIGHT, INC.—for the poems of Hart Crane from *The Collected Poems of Hart Crane*, copyright 1933 by Liveright, Inc.

THE MACMILLAN CO.—for poems of Tristram Coffin from *Collected Poems* by Tristram Coffin, copyright

copyright 1938 by New Directions; for "Sunday In the Park" from *Paterson, Book II* by William Carlos Williams, copyright 1948 by William Carlos Williams; and for the poems of Yvor Winters from *The Giant Weapon* by Yvor Winters, copyright 1943 by New Directions.

THE NEW YORKER MAGAZINE and JOHN HOLMES —for "The Overgrown Back Yard" by John Holmes, copyright 1953 by *The New Yorker* Magazine, Inc.

NOONDAY PRESS—for the poems of Louise Bogan from *Collected Poems* by Louise Bogan, copyright 1954 by Louise Bogan.

OXFORD UNIVERSITY PRESS—for poems of Conrad Aiken from *Collected Poems* by Conrad Aiken, copyright 1953 by Conrad Aiken; for "Ah (you say), this is Holy Wisdom" from *Tribute To Angels* by H. D., copyright 1945 by Oxford University Press; for "Ode to the Chinese Paper Snake" from *Selected Poems* by Richard Eberhardt and "The Horse Chestnut Tree" from *Undercliff* by Richard Eberhardt.

KENNETH PATCHEN—for his poems from *Orchards, Thrones, and Caravans* by Kenneth Patchen (Print Workshop, San Francisco).

NORMAN HOLMES PEARSON—for "An Incident Here and There" from *The Walls Do Not Fall* by H. D. (Oxford, 1944).

DACHINE RAINER—for her poem.

RANDOM HOUSE INC.—for poem of Paul Engle from *The Word of Love* by Paul Engle, copyright 1951 by Paul Engle; for "Summer Holliday" from *Roan Stallion, Tamar and Other Poems* by Robinson Jeffers, copyright renewed 1953 by Robinson Jeffers, "Reference to a Passage in Plutarch's Life of Sulla" from *Dear Judas* by Robinson Jeffers, copyright 1929 by Robinson Jeffers, "November Surf" from *Thurso's Landing* by Robinson Jeffers, copyright 1938 by Robinson Jeffers, "I Shall Laugh Purely" from *Be Angry at the Sun* by Robinson Jeffers, copyright 1941 by Robinson Jeffers, and "The Eye" from *The Double Axe and Other Poems* by Robinson Jeffers, copyright 1948 by Robinson Jeffers; for poems of Karl Shapiro from *Person, Place and Thing* by Karl Shapiro, copyright 1942 by Karl Jay Shapiro; for "To Daphne and Virginia" from *The Desert Music and Other Poems* by William Carlos Williams, copyright 1954 by William Carlos Williams.

RINEHART & CO.—for poem of John Gould Fletcher from *Selected Poems* by John Gould Fletcher, copyright 1938 by John Gould Fletcher.

CHARLES SCRIBNER'S SONS—for poem of John Peale Bishop from *The Collected Poems of John Peale Bishop*, copyright 1948 by Charles Scribner's Sons; for "The Cynneddf" (first published in *The New Yorker*) and "Render Unto Caesar" from *Poems, Collected and New* by Rolfe Humphries, copyright 1945, 1949 by Rolfe Humphries; for "Clavering" from *The Town Down the River* by Edwin Arlington Robinson, copyright 1910 by Charles Scribner's Sons, 1938 by Ruth Nivison; for "Seasons of the Soul" from *Poems 1922-1947* by Allan Tate, copyright 1948 by Charles Scribner's Sons; for poem of Peter Viereck from *Strike Through the Mask!* by Peter Viereck, copyright 1950 by Peter Viereck; and for poems of John Hall Wheelock from *Poems Old and New* by John Hall Wheelock, copyright 1927, 1936 by John Hall Wheelock.

HENRY L. STICKNEY—for poems of Trumbull Stickney from *The Poems of Trumbull Stickney* (Houghton Mifflin, 1905).

ALAN SWALLOW—for poems of Janet Lewis from *Poems 1924-1944* by Janet Lewis, copyright 1950 by Janet Lewis.

ALLEN TATE—for "The Buried Lake," first published in the *Sewanee Review*, Spring 1953.

TWAYNE PUBLISHERS—for "What Does a Man Think About" from "Water Poem" in *The Double Root* by John Holmes; and for the poems of Merrill Moore from *Illegitimate Sonnets* by Merrill Moore.

MARK VAN DOREN—for his poems from *Collected Poems* by Mark Van Doren (Henry Holt and Co.).

CARL VAN VECHTEN—for poems of Gertrude Stein from *Last Operas and Plays* by Gertrude Stein (Rinehart, 1949).

VIKING PRESS—for poems of Horace Gregory from *Selected Poems of Horace Gregory*, copyright 1951 by Horace Gregory; for "Country Club Sunday" (first published in *The New Yorker*) from *A Short Walk to the Station* by Phyllis McGinley, copyright 1946, 1951 by Phyllis McGinley, and "Portrait of a Girl With a Comic Book" (first published in *The New Yorker*) from *The Love Letters of Phyllis McGinley*, copyright 1952, 1954 by Phyllis McGinley; for poem of Dorothy Parker from *The Portable Dorothy Parker*, copyright 1927, 1944 by Dorothy Parker; for poems of José Garcia Villa from *Have Come, Am Here* by José Garcia Villa, copyright 1941, 1942 by José Garcia Villa.

ROBERT PENN WARREN—for his poems from *Collected Poems 1923-1943* by Robert Penn Warren, copyright 1944 by Robert Penn Warren (Harcourt, Brace).

INDEX OF AUTHORS

INDEX OF FIRST LINES

A is to begin with, and A began with Adam, 302
A man adrift on a slim spar, 34
A man said to the universe, 34
A passer-by might just as well be blind, 211
A realm is here of masquing light, 203
A slant-windowed, belt-footed enormously long-boomed, 228
A wet day on the road: the slim blades cutting, 258
Above the fresh ruffles of the surf, 187
After a banquet, 162
After the centres' naked files, the basic line, 276
Ah (you say), this is Holy Wisdom, 108
All our stones like as much sun as possible, 262
Always alone, star told? 149
American muse, whose strong and diverse heart, 174
An agitation of the air, 239
An incident here and there, 106
Another armoured animal—scale, 126
An underground grower, blind and a common brown, 307
And still the picknickers come on, now, 79
And the day arrives at last, my friends, 304
At four o'clock, 267
At midnight, in the garden never planted, 221
At the first stepping-stone, the past of water, 139
At the foot of a great pine, in the wild country, 112
At Rochecourt, 93
Authors and actors and artists and such, 150

Back out of all this now too much for us, 51
Beasts in their major freedom, 308
Beautiful as the flying legend of some leopard, 134
Be beautiful, noble, like the antique ant, 247
Before remembrance we moved here, 204
Bethou me, said sparrow, to the crackled blade, 76
Between God's eyelashes I look at you, 247
Bewildered with the broken tongue, 147
Blue sky, blue noon, and the secret line is flung, 140
boss i just discovered what, 54

Boys in sporadic but tenacious droves, 233
By a peninsula the painter sat and, 148
By dark severance the apparition head, 135

Chameleon, knowing I am near, 249
Complacencies of the peignoir, and late, 70
Cowhorn-crowned, shockheaded, cornshuck-bearded, 277
Created by the poet to sing my song, 299

Darkness has called to darkness, and disgrace, 294
Dead, they'll burn you up with electricity, 236
Death threshholded old man hold, 311
Dürer would have seen a reason for living, 119

England with its baby rivers and little towns, 123
Eternal Spirit, you, 205

Factory windows are always broken, 67
Faintly the ne'er-do-well, 58
Far down the purple wood, 264
Five geese deploy mysteriously, 57
For three years, out of key with his time, 99
From loud sound and still chance, 169

Go and ask Robin to bring the girls over, 131
Go to the western gate, Luke Havergal, 28

had a great ride boss, 55
He knew how Roman legions looked, for he, 145
He runs before the wise men: He, 238
He thought he kept the universe alone, 49
He would declare and could himself believe, 50
Held on the slightest of bamboo poles, 230
Here dock and tare, 142
Here is a face that says half-past seven, 56
How many dawns, chill from his rippling rest, 184
How still, how very still the air is, 180

I feel myself like the flame, 208
I found a dimpled spider, fat and white, 48
I lived a life without love, and saw the being, 209

The beautiful American word, Sure, 274
The bench, the sewermouth, the hydrant placed, 223
The blue, faded purple, horizon mount, 148
The calloused grass lies hard, 205
The Dai horse neighs against the bleak wind of Etsu, 96
The daughters of the horseleech, crying 'Give! Give!, 238
The end of everything approaches, 90
The furious prisoner of the womb, 284
The heavy bear who goes with me, 273
The houses are haunted, 69
The hunchback on the corner, with gum and shoelaces, 244
The land was overmuch like scenery, 309
The long, long legs, 266
The mind is an enchanting thing, 129
The moon rises. The red cubs rolling, 276
The north-east wind was the wind off the lake, 146
The people along the sand, 48
The people buying and selling, consuming pleasures, 113
The road at the top of the rise, 50
The sky is perfectly clear, 235
The smell of the heat is boxwood, 86
The Sphinx with lion's feet, 213
The stethoscope tells what everyone fears, 251
The sun is blue and scarlet on my page, 295
The whisky on your breath, 251
The windmills, like great sunflowers of steel, 104
Then touch the park: the leaves are stained to lure you, 288
There are too many heart-shaped words for one, 226
There is a rumour hereabout of summer, 228
There is a singer everyone has heard, 43
There was no repose, 300
There was such speed in her little body, 131
Thin air I breathe and birds use for flying, 223
Think of the storm roaming the sky uneasily, 272
Thirteen's no age at all, 241
This age it is the same/with less remembered, 225
This dim and Ptolemaic man, 144
This is the place, as wild as summer snow, 289
Thus systole addressed diastole, 138
Time cannot break the bird's wing from the bird, 143